Making A Broadway Musical

Making It Run

MAKING A BROADWAY MUSICAL

MAKING IT RUN

An Anatomy of Entrepreneurship

by

John D. Mitchell

Cover Illustration by Caissa Douwes

Northwood Institute Press
Midland, Michigan 48640

First Edition

© 1989 by Northwood Institute Press

All rights reserved, including the right of reproduction in whole or in part, in any form or by any means, electronic or mechanical, including photocopying, recording, or by any information storage and retrieval system, without permission in writing from the publisher. Inquiries should be addressed to Northwood Institute Press, Midland, Michigan 48640.

LCN 89-062889   ISBN 0—87359-049-X

Printed in the United States of America

DEDICATION

To my sister Beulah who made it possible for me, as a young man, to climb Mount Everest with my fingernails – New York.

TABLE OF CONTENTS

ACKNOWLEDGEMENTS

INTRODUCTION

CHAPTER I	Ken: A Five-Year-Old Who Wants to be Boss.	1
CHAPTER II	Maxine: A Six-Year-Old Who Wants to Dance.	7
CHAPTER III	Ken: Moving and Shaking on Campus.	11
CHAPTER IV	Maxine: Quitting College for Show Business.	19
CHAPTER V	Ken: Producing TV in South America.	23
CHAPTER VI	Maxine: From Girl Friday to Company Manager.	31
CHAPTER VII	Ken and Maxine: Getting Their Feet Wet Producing.	43
CHAPTER VIII	Ken and Maxine: Discovering GREASE in a Basement.	51
CHAPTER IX	Ken and Maxine: A Setback with OVER HERE!.	75
CHAPTER X	GREASE Becomes a Top-Grossing Movie.	83
CHAPTER XI	How to Produce a Show	95

RESIDUUM ... 111
EPILOGUE. ... 115
SELECTED BIBLIOGRAPHY. ... 117
FILMS - MATERIALS - BACKGROUND ... 118
ORDERS AND INQUIRIES ... 123
INDEX ... 125

FOREWORD

Entrepreneurship has enabled Broadway to excel in the productions of musicals as well as plays. To the admiration of the whole world the long run musical became an American phenomenon. Today, from Tokyo to Paris — even on occasion Moscow — producers in these world capitals follow Broadway openings, the critic's assessments of these shows, as well as noting accolades earned as symbolized by the Tony Awards.

At the tender ages of 31 and 27 respectively Kenneth Waissman and Maxine Fox proved to be successful theatre entrepreneurs. Their musical phenomenon GREASE, until quite recently, enjoyed the record of the longest running Broadway show (play or musical) in history. Ironically, a Broadway producer had suggested they keep GREASE at the Eden Theatre downtown on Second Avenue. It's another dimension of entrepreneurship to listen to another Broadway producer's advice, but then go ahead and make an independent decision. Had they kept GREASE downtown, they may not have ever surpassed an all-time record-breaking run of FIDDLER ON THE ROOF.

A year after GREASE opened, composers Richard and Robert Sherman approached Ken and Maxine with an idea for a Big Band, World War II home front musical. The Waissmans were excited by the Sherman Brothers' idea and the result was the musical OVER HERE!, which brought back to public awareness the Andrews Sisters. In some respects OVER HERE! demonstrated more dramatically and vividly a special kind of entrepreneurship. From little more than an idea, Ken and Maxine, with their colleagues in the theatre developed a major theatre event. Much water had gone over the dam since the end of World War II, but they daringly showed that nostalgia brilliantly produced could not only win over the critics but could fill a Broadway theatre. Husbands and wives who had enjoyed the big bands of the war years were joined by a new generation discovering the pleasures of the big brass sound and the Andrews Sisters.

I'm told that the day in Sardi's when the author of this book proposed telling their story and the story of GREASE, Ken and Maxine almost with one voice said in response to the suggestion "but, we're so young." I like that, because it denotes not only humility, but highlights something that is uniquely American; youth is no barrier to entrepreneurship.

It pleases me that this story of Broadway production is being published by Northwood Institute Press with the goal of making this informative book available to young college and university students in our 50 states. This is not fiction, and telling it like it is undoubtedly can inspire as well as encourage American youth that it is still possible, in theatre as well as elsewhere, to be an entrepreneur.

Dr. David E. Fry
President
Northwood Institute

ACKNOWLEDGMENTS

Among the many who have been supportive of this book are Arthur E. Turner and R. Gary Stauffer. One could almost imagine that they, as founders of Northwood Institute, had been the first to coin for the English language the word entrepreneur. As such, they created a dynamic educational institution; they invited the Institute for Advanced Studies in the Theatre Arts (IASTA) to work in association with Northwood Institute to create a Musical Theatre Studio to which Ken Waissman and Maxine Fox of this book contributed richly of their talent.

Much thanks is due to Ken and Maxine, always very busy entrepreneurs. They cheerfully gave over hours to being interviewed and to reading over the manuscript of this book.

Turning now to a friend of very many years, I find words fail me to express adequately my thanks and acknowledgment of his enormous editorial contribution to the work. I write of George Eells who happened not only to have been a schoolmate, but a favorite author as well. Each of his theatre and film biographies has been looked forward to by me, eagerly, and several I've read more than once. If this book has resulted in desired terseness and lucidity, very, very much is due to his keen eye and ear.

Robert Epstein and George Drew, as colleagues and friends of many years, very generously devoted numerous hours seeking out misspelled words and lapses in continuity. Another friend and colleague, Richard Philp, shared his enthusiasm for the book and contributed to the title.

I am a goal-centered person, but without the enthusiasm and encouragement of my wife Miriam, my three children and their spouses, my colleague and dear friend Mary W. John, and my most patient and steadfast assistant Gil Forman, I think by the third rewrite, I might have shelved this book.

Over an extended period Irene Shawtell, as secretary, typed up miles of taped studio sessions and interviews, for which I am grateful.

Thanks are due to Melodie Greer and Michael Guerette for their secretarial assistance.

Virginia Morrison, editor of Northwood Institute Press, has been ever helpful, nurturing the book from inception to a printed and bound book.

Ken Waissman & Maxine Fox

INTRODUCTION

Kenneth Waissman and Maxine Fox, both coming from the city of Baltimore, achieved recognition, riches, and became Broadway's youngest producers.

I had invited them to lunch with me at Sardi's, the theatrical restaurant. The year was 1980. As I waited at their table for that first lunch with them, the maitre d'hotel, Jimmie, alerted me as to which place at the table was Ken's, which was Maxine's. Ken seated himself in his; Maxine in hers, enabling each of them to see and be seen as the elite of Broadway entered the restaurant.

Even in repose, the two of them are, one senses, bundles of nervous energy. Both are close to being of the same height; Ken admits to having once been self-conscious of being short. As he nodded his head, crowned with brown, curly hair, there was no evidence this day of self-consciousness, as he greeted theatre acquaintances. Maxine's luminous eyes bespoke her strong-mindedness, although as our conversation progressed she'd say what she had to say, often deferring to Ken.

I hadn't remembered that our paths had crossed earlier. Ken and Maxine had rehearsed their production of Sal Mineo's version of FORTUNE AND MEN'S EYES in a space they had rented from the Institute for Advanced Studies in the Theatre Arts (IASTA) then on New York's 42nd Street.

My real awareness of them began with their participation as Masters from Broadway in IASTA's Musical Theatre Studios on the Northwood Institute campus near Dallas, Texas. (This made them accessible to me.)

Ken told the story of GREASE, entertainingly, as might a stand-up comedian, and each told his and her view of show business on Broadway with joy and spontaneity. They seemed to have almost total recall and complete rapport with young, emerging, professional musical theatre performers. They had heart, to quote from a classic Broadway song.

Without much preliminary I said to both of them over lunch, "I want to write your biography, to write about both of you."

At first they protested, "But we're so young..."

I countered with, "Noel Coward during his long life in the theatre wrote three autobiographies; John Gielgud has done two or more over the years." The pause was becoming less than theatrical and more like an uncomfortable stage-wait.

Having come to Sardi's prepared, I drew from my brief case first one book, then another book, and still another book; all of which I had written and had published. I assumed I had to convince them that I wrote and that a publisher was interested.

After a pause, Maxine looked at Ken, saying, "You make the decision."

I had no idea of what might be making them hesitate. I began to feel nervous. I said truthfully, "It's entrepreneurship that interests me, your encouraging young people to be entrepreneurs."

Ken said, as he looked at Maxine, "Let's do it."

Their success (no accident) was, I felt, deserving of a book. New York Senator Moynihan had read into the Congressional Record an imposing tribute to them: "Mr. President, the American musical GREASE became the longest running show in the history of Broadway on the evening of December 8, 1979, with its 3,243rd performance, surpassing FIDDLER ON THE ROOF which played 3,242 performances from September 22, 1964, through July 2, 1972.

"GREASE, set in the 1950's, portrays adolescence and the universal growing pains that every generation experiences. Since it opened in New York at the Eden Theatre on February 14, 1972, it has introduced to the public a whole new generation of young stage, film and television stars, including such celebrated names as Adrienne Barbeau, Barry Bostwick, Jeff Conaway, Candice Early, Greg Evigan, Richard Gere, Randy Heller, Marilu Henner, Judy Kaye, Ilene Kristen, Rex Smith, John Travolta, Chick Vennera, Ted Wass and Treat Williams. The play is a triumph also for its director, Tom Moore; choreographer, Patricia Birch; composers and authors, Jim Jacobs and Warren Casey and for its producers, Kenneth Waissman and Maxine Fox.

"In March of 1972, GREASE received seven nominations for the American Theatre Wing's Antoinette Perry Awards (Broadway's equivalent of Hollywood's Academy Awards).

"On June 7, 1972, the production moved to the Broadhurst Theatre on 44th Street and on November 21, 1972, moved once again to the Royale Theatre on 45th Street, which has been its home ever since. On December 23, 1972, Waissman and Fox sent out the first National Touring Company of GREASE. Since then, nine touring companies have crisscrossed the United States and Canada.

"The large number of return engagements (seven) caused a Washington, D.C. drama critic to comment, 'We look forward to this show each season. A year without GREASE is like a year without the circus.'

"Total gross in the United States on Waissman and Fox productions of GREASE New York and national companies is approximately $70,000,000. Capitalized at $110,000., the musical thus far returned a 4,000%[1] profit to its investors.

"The film version released by Paramount Pictures on June 13, 1978, starred Olivia Newton-John and former Broadway cast member John Travolta. The film has grossed approximately $200,000,000[2].

"Other Waissman and Fox productions include the musical OVER HERE! which starred the Andrews Sisters, AND MISS REARDON DRINKS A LITTLE which starred Julie Harris and Estelle Parsons, and FORTUNE AND MEN'S EYES directed by the late Sal Mineo. The Waissmans produced the entertainment for New York's salute to Congress October 10, 1979, at the Washington Hilton. They also produced the all-star V.I.P. NIGHT ON BROADWAY at the Shubert Theatre, April 22, 1979, which netted $150,000 for the purchase of bulletproof vests for New York's policemen."

Success is an American dream, and I have sought from Ken and Maxine, separately now, the roots in their childhood of their dreams for success to be entrepreneurs, and telling the story of making a Broadway musical and making it run.

---

[1] This percentage has increased over the years to over 10,000%.
[2] Subsequently, additional income from television, video sales and the soundtrack album, has greatly increased this figure.

The French verb *entreprendre*, from which we in English get entrepreneur, translates as: to undertake, to take in hand. This book is an anatomy of entrepreneurship.

Increasingly today the world is one of computers, conglomerates, and satellite communication. The poet and writer, the painter, the composer are almost solely those who 'take in hand' their work and produce an end product. Theatre has always been a handmade group effort, and it seems to many an anachronism in today's microchip world. It is an art, and despite collaboration, it cannot be mass produced. So here there is a role for entrepreneurs.

Also, the story of Ken Waissman and Maxine Fox seems reassuring that entrepreneurship may still prevail in the United States, despite big business, big unions, big government.

Thinking, then, of the long-run musical GREASE, I asked both Ken and Maxine, "How did it all begin?"

"In a basement in Chicago," replied Maxine.

"In a basement?"

"Yes, GREASE began in a basement in Chicago."

"Ah, yes," I replied, "but we'll get back to that later."

I am customarily disposed to start an action at a high and climactic point of interest, but as I came to know them through hours of interviews, I realized that the roots of their ambitions manifested themselves dramatically at a tender age.

Let's get the curtain up! How did it all begin for Ken? How did it begin for Maxine?

John D. Mitchell

John D. Mitchell, EdD; HHD (HC)
President
Institute for Advanced Studies in the
    Theatre Arts (IASTA)

CHAPTER ONE

Ken Waissman was five years old when he saw the Broadway musical FINIAN'S RAINBOW. The baby-sitter had suddenly been taken ill, so Ken's parents took him with them to New York from Baltimore and, with some misgivings, they took their five-year-old with them to see his first show.

"Who's the boss?" asked Ken of his father as they left the theatre after the performance of FINIAN'S RAINBOW.

"My father replied," "The boss of a Broadway show is a producer." Ken said right off, "Then, I want to be a producer."

Later, that grandiose ambition didn't scare Ken's kindergarten teacher, but it stunned her and the class. The teacher had asked each of the children what they were going to be when they had grown up.

"For me, there was an incredible magic to FINIAN'S RAINBOW. I don't even know if I can verbalize it. I remember sitting there watching; it was the first time I had ever seen a stage show. It wasn't a movie; these people were real. I was so caught up in its magic. It was a feeling of being outside of my little, immediate environment as a five-year-old. It was the most significant thing that had happened to me. I think a lot about it. Why did I get fired with the love of theatre? There had been other children taken to see FINIAN'S RAINBOW. They may have absolutely loved it, but it did not become for them their whole life. My feelings at five were very strong. I was very impressed by things, things that were large, people who were famous, anything that was famous.

"New York, to me, was like that, because it was so famous. At five I had heard about New York; my parents had talked about it.

"This show had a magic that was being created there on stage while I was sitting there. My impression of Broadway was that everything was perfect. The 46th Street Theatre was a grand place. The house curtain, which I reacted to when I walked in, was elegant. The

46th Street Theatre was in very good condition then. It reeked of expense, importance, fame. The magic being created on stage affected all the people sitting there in the theatre. It gave me a heightened sense.

"I now think that part of my being taken with theatre had to do with my very strict upbringing. It was very, very strict. Oddly, mother was not quite as strict with my sister as she was with me. Whatever the doctor said, that was it. If he said at one year old I was to be in bed by 6:30, I was in bed by 6:30; not 6:31. I felt constricted in my environment.

"What could I do? I couldn't fire them and hire two more parents, or go on strike. At that age maybe I could have gone on strike, I didn't think of it. It made my parents seem very important. Somewhere there was a feeling that I wanted to be more important than my parents, and on a grand scale.

"Staying up late was a real treat, exciting. Small wonder that I sat there feeling mesmerized by the magic of FINIAN'S RAINBOW. It was providential, I think, that FINIAN'S RAINBOW was the first. I may have reacted differently if BORN YESTERDAY had been first, if OKLAHOMA had been the first. (That weekend I saw all three shows with my folks.) FINIAN'S RAINBOW had a kind of magic in the working out of the story that a young child could relate to. There was fairy-tale quality about it. I remember I was so taken with the lighting, the colored lights, the scenery. The more artificial and more painted the scenery looked, the more exciting it was for me. It was make-believe! The backdrop of FINIAN'S RAINBOW was fields of different patterns, an obviously painted background, a large papier-mache tree where the characters hide the gold. There were Leprechauns and a girl that couldn't speak but communicated through dancing."

Ken has not seen FINIAN'S RAINBOW since then. Interesting how detailed his memory of it was. I saw it as an adult, and Ken remembers more about it than I do. He was five years old.

"I do remember very clearly the entrance of Finian and his daughter," Ken went on. "I remember where she stood on the stage when she sang How Are Things In Glockamora. I remember feeling frightened when she changed the senator into a black man, the way it was done with lightning and noise. I was really scared. But along with being scared was my enjoyment of the power to do that to someone. As well as the power of the stage to make people laugh, make people be scared, make people applaud, make people be excited.

CHAPTER ONE

"Who's the boss? is what I asked as we were leaving the 46th Street Theatre. Yes, I was thinking and expressing what I felt as I sat there watching the show.

"I'll never forget OKLAHOMA. (I did see a revival of OKLAHOMA as an adult and it brought back a certain kind of nostalgia.) I remember that we arrived late to see OKLAHOMA and the overture was just about over. The curtain went up, and Aunt Eller was there churning the butter. Curly comes on and sings Oh What A Beautiful Morning. Ironically, when I went to see the revival at the Palace Theatre in New York, I was late again and walked into the theatre as Aunt Eller was sitting there churning butter. I've yet to see OKLAHOMA with the overture!"

Years later, in Dallas, Texas, at the time of the Musical Theatre Studio of IASTA, Ken had a meeting with Yip Harburg.

"I felt a childlike awe," said Ken, "sitting and talking with the man who had written the lyrics to FINIAN'S RAINBOW, the first show I'd ever seen. What was it about these shows that started me on a course leading to theatre? The performers and authors were not in my life. Then to come full circle and to be sitting with Yip Harburg, talking with him critically, was a connection that had been made. It was a good feeling, a feeling to be invited to do the critique of Yip's work. True, at first I felt inhibited. But once I got into it, he was no longer Yip Harburg who had written the lyrics to FINIAN'S RAINBOW. He was now just a human being in the business; we were having a discussion. I was impressed with the way he reacted to some of the things I had to say. It was an interesting exchange on a peer level. I found it very gratifying. I thoroughly enjoyed the three hours we talked.

"My father always preached that sticking up for what you wanted was important and not to worry about whether you're going to be liked! Only worry about whether you're going to be respected for what you're doing.

"I had my parents' moral support and their challenges. My first challenge occurred when I was in kindergarten. I loved graham crackers at school, because they were something I couldn't get at home. We didn't have anything like that around. The house was void of sweets and 'junk' food most of the time. I hated milk because I had to drink four glasses of milk a day. That was a rule of the house. A quart of milk until I had been graduated from high school!

"So to have to suffer through milk in school was outrageous. Of course, I wouldn't drink the milk. So the teacher said — she knew I liked the graham crackers — 'If you don't drink the milk, you're not going to get the Graham crackers.'

"So I went through an entire year of kindergarten during the recess having no milk...or Graham crackers. I wasn't going to give in, and I didn't.

"I was challenging the teacher all the time. I found how easy it was to win. But I never could break down my parents. I just couldn't. I could never bring them to a point of tears or a point of frustration. But, I found that other grown-ups were easy targets.

"The kindergarten teacher called home again when I refused to draw pictures of our school yard or our coming to school."

To draw him out, I asked Ken, "What was that all about?"

"Well, I was fascinated at that time with Jesus Christ," said Ken. "Our next door neighbor was a very religious lady. She was Roman Catholic. I'd go over and sit on her porch and talk with her. Here I was, a Jewish tot, talking about Catholicism and everything about Jesus Christ. I'd asked her, 'What does He look like?' One day she showed me a picture that she had cut out of a newspaper. I thought, 'It's like seeing God in person.'

"So in kindergarten I would only draw Jesus Christ. Sometimes some angels with Him. That's all I would do.

"No matter what teachers would say to me, I would not draw anything else. There were times when the teacher would see me start to draw, and she'd pull the drawing paper away from me. She'd say, 'When you're ready to draw...' I would just sit there, and I wouldn't draw anything.

"The climax came in the first grade. The first grade were to draw a 'movie' that was to be shown to the second grade. The 'movie' was a cardboard box with a window in it. The pictures which the kids had drawn were then pasted together on a roller. That was the movie: first one rolls up one drawing and then another and another drawing.

"The theme for the 'movie' was back to school. Each child was to draw a picture on that theme. All submitted their pictures. One was of two kids standing with a book bag, another kid by a tree, another a schoolhouse under a sky with a sun. This was what the kids had been asked to draw.

"I submitted my picture; Jesus Christ with an angel. The teacher said, 'That's not the theme. We're not going to use it.'

"I threw such a tantrum and carried on to such an extent that finally she said, 'We'll use the picture."

"Then what happened?" I asked.

"My first grade teacher was Miss Jett, who looked to me as if she were a hundred feet in the air; teachers sometimes have names that go with their looks. For the second grade, she was showing the 'movie', rolling the drawings, and she'd say, 'This 'picture' is by so-and-so and it's a boy and a girl on their way to school on their first day. You can see their book bags, and this is two school children playing on a swing at school, and you can see the school back there. 'She kept going and explaining. Suddenly, up comes my drawing. Miss Jett said, 'This is a picture of Jesus Christ', and real quick she moves on. I felt so embarrassed. I realized how inappropriate it was, how absolutely absurd. Never again did I insist on drawing pictures of Jesus Christ and angels."

Ken found insight in that childhood rebellion, saying "Fascination with Him was obviously the fact that Jesus Christ was all powerful. He was God, and there were no strict parents telling Him what he could or couldn't do. That to me, was incredible, that you could be that free and that nobody could tell you what to do. He had that much power."

"Ken pondered, "Is this the whole motivation of...? Why did I want to be a producer?" Ken has asked himself. "Why did I choose a career of pulling creative people together and making something happen out of nothing? Why?

"As a small child there were no other children around. That might have contributed to my feeling of smallness. Physically, I was smaller than other kids my age. Mentally, I think, I felt tiny, too. I would just listen to adult conversation or play by myself, inventing a whole world of people. My mother has said sometimes I would be out on the porch and it would sound as if there were ten kids out there. She'd walk out and there would be just me. You know with my soldiers, my war tanks.

"There was no television. I have no memory of other radio programs; I do remember the evening news. I used to get scared to death whenever the news came on. It took me many years to figure out why. I was too young to be interested in World War II news, but when the news came on I lost the attention of my parents, it was as if I didn't exist. They were glued to that radio. For years and years, all through college, I used to hate radio news. If I were in a car when the news came on, I'd immediately switch to something else. A first big disappointment in my young life was when my mother told me that when the war was over there was still going to be 'news.' There would still be news? What kind of news could there be when the war was over? I wanted the war to be over for one reason and one reason only. So there wouldn't have to be any more news!"

When he wasn't much older than seven, shows became the big thing in Ken's life. With the neighborhood kids, he staged plays in the family basement. Each successive production became more imposing. Not content with 'amateur' productions for which he was the boss, Ken auditioned and became a regular on a children's program for the local Baltimore television station. It was titled THE CANDY CORNER and produced by Bert Claster who later created ROMPER ROOM.

One morning, Ken was down with a cold, running a fairly high temperature. From someone Ken had heard the dictum that 'the show must go on', as well as 'no excuses.' At first, his parents were adamant that he not go out with a fever. Ken's protestations that he had to go on began to border on hysteria. The family doctor was called in. He recognized the risk of exciting the child more; he calmed the parents, urged them to bundle up Ken well, and get him to the station in a warm car.

"I did go on," said Ken. I couldn't conceive of missing the show. Maybe that has an indication of my becoming a showbusiness entrepreneur.

CHAPTER TWO

When Maxine Fox was six she was taken to a performance of a ballet in her hometown of Baltimore. She informed her parents afterwards, "I want to be a dancer." Shortly thereafter, she took her first dancing lesson. Her parents were not in theatre; both were in advertising.

"Some people," said Maxine, "called Dad the greatest actor in the world. It's not so surprising, to me, that I'm in show business. He would go into an office and mesmerize the heads of major corporations, radio and television stations. He was a very flamboyant man.

"Dad had always told me that the best people hang out in New York; not Baltimore — Baltimore was small potatoes."

Still I felt I knew less about Maxine than I wanted to know. I wanted to explore with her on the level of feelings, her growing up and gravitation toward show business.

"Since your earliest ambition had been to be a dancer," I asked, "when did you start dancing and how deep was your commitment?"

Maxine replied, "I started when I was about six years old. Early on I was involved emotionally in music, in one way or another. I made a choice in first grade. The teacher asked me, 'Do you want to join the others on the farm trip or stay in school and take a dance class?' I chose the dance class.

"It was always show business in one aspect or another."

"Actors talk of those waves of love coming up over the footlights to them as they are performing," I commented.

"That wasn't what I wanted. I was scared to death as a performer. It was not the performance in front of an audience. It was the joy within my own body. It was to achieve it for myself, all of it.

"As far back as I can remember I loved the feeling I got from moving my body.

"I remember doing a rhythmic ballet. I remember doing PETER AND THE WOLF. In Baltimore, there was a very good dance teacher from Russia. I began taking ballet lessons from him. I was always one of the best in his classes. I loved it. I remember simply feeling joy and looking forward to going to class. Dance classes were a special pleasure of my growing up."

"How did your family feel about that?" I interrupted.

"My family was totally supportive. They got me there on time. They always gave me the feeling that I was special."

"Early in your childhood, the Ballets Russes played Baltimore?" I asked.

"The Ballets Russes had come to town, and the director of the Ballets Russes gave the studio I attended a special master class. I remember the warm-ups and all of us scattered along at the barre. The director from the Ballets Russes was barking instructions at some of the other students, seeming to ignore me. When class was over, I was in tears. I was convinced he didn't like me. Here, I had been considered one of the best dancers in my age group, and suddenly this 'god' from across the ocean paid no attention to me whatsoever. I was in the dressing room crying my eyes out. My mother was there trying to console me. Here comes the Russian into the dressing room, comes over to me with my teacher and says to him in front of me, 'That little one. I didn't correct her, because she didn't need correction!' Here I thought I wasn't good enough!"

Maxine's family went to Atlantic City every summer. At their hotel she took classes given by one of the dancers who performed in the hotel club.

"I had something that people were attracted to. One of the dancers asked my parents if he could put together a routine for me to perform with him and his partner as a night club act. My parents agreed. [In Maxine's words, he went crazy about her talent. She was 11 years old.] That night I froze completely. I had been dynamite in rehearsals, but on opening night, I forgot half the routines. I was winging it all the way. My father and mother still remember the relief they felt. They thought my failure was the best thing for me then."

Sometime after that, the dancer called Maxine's father in Baltimore and told him that he wanted him to bring her to New York to work with him. He had choreographed another piece for Maxine.

CHAPTER TWO

"I've always been closer to the choreographer of a show than to the director or to the writers or to the music director. I respond to the way someone moves in a show I'm producing.

"I love sports; I love dance; I love the body doing beautiful movements. A 50-yard pass in a football game; a basket in a basketball game; a back flip in gymnastics. All show form. I love the aesthetics of form. But I wanted to go and play baseball, not practice at the barre before a mirror downstairs in a basement.

"Some people in the world make it, and success has to come from somewhere. My Dad was in my success somewhere.

"He was a man and a superb salesman. He was the best. What he sold was an idea, and he did it unconventionally. He was talented, powerful, and would only talk to the president of a company. He would demand a half an hour of his time and insist on a 'yes' or 'no' at the end of the presentation.

"'I have to walk out of this meeting with a signed contract — and a check!' Dad did not know the words 'you can't.'

"My brother came along, and he was slow in some areas, so my father invested in me. He really wanted me to try it on my own as he would have wanted a son to do."

Maxine's father died a year or so before that shatteringly successful night of December 8, 1979, when GREASE had established for its time the longest run of a Broadway show.

"My mother is 83 now. When she was in her twenties she and my father became partners in the advertising business and Mom was one of the highest paid women in that field, unheard of for a woman at that time.

"I had two remarkable role models; Mom and Dad. I was given a leg up. I may have suffered for it in other ways."

9

CHAPTER THREE

While in senior high school, Ken put together a Junior Day assembly program. It was a tradition for parents, members of the School Board, and the head of the Board of Education of Baltimore to attend. It was always a big deal. A girl and Ken were selected to become co-directors of the program. "We decided to do BALLAD FOR AMERICANS," said Ken. We were trying to cast it, trying to get the junior class involved. But no one could sing the lead.

"Since the age of ten, I had been singing on a television show in Baltimore. While in high school, I had earned money singing with one of the local orchestras around town. Already at this point in my life I wasn't interested in performing. I had been as a kid. Now, I was experiencing the surge of fulfillment, a sense of being alive through putting on shows. Performing couldn't compare with producing, even in a basement theatre or at the High School.

"I was excited about co-directing and co-producing Junior Day. The principal came to me and said, 'There's no one in the class who can sing the lead.

The music teacher said, 'You are going to have to do it, Ken.'

Ken said, 'Okay, on one condition. I'm not giving up the directing, but I will sing the lead.'

"About a week from presentation — less than a week away, I happened to see a copy of the program. I saw that I was listed as a soloist, but I was not listed as director at all. Only the girl was. I went to the principal; I went to the head of the music department; and to the class advisor; and I said, 'You know, I only agreed to perform on one condition. Since I no longer enjoy performing, I told you I would not give up being co-director of the assembly.' "

"They maintained that Ken had to face reality, that there were some students in the junior class that didn't have any role in the program, that one person's having two jobs was really unfair. They had decided that they wouldn't allow it.

Ken replied, "Oh, so in the interest of fairness and because some students couldn't be involved at all, then, nobody can be involved in more than one job? Okay, I'll agree to that. So now I'm the director, and I will not be doing the singing."

"They went crazy,' Ken said. "They told me, 'You're going to lose all your friends. Everybody is going to hate you."

Ken said, "I don't care."

"I was told repeatedly I was being uncooperative; I'd never get through life unless I learned how to be fair, to try to get along along with people. Where was my school spirit?

"They went on and on. I was called to the principal's office. I was called into the music teacher's office."

"Ken said, "I'm sorry. We made a deal. You broke it. I have no voice anymore. I won't be at rehearsal today. That's it."

Ken enjoyed relating the climax of the event, "I didn't go to rehearsal. The next day they reprinted the program listing me as soloist and co-director."

I asked Ken, "Where did all this mature, toughness of mind come from? As early as high school?"

Ken feels it came from his parents, and perhaps mostly from his mother whose background was German-Jewish. "German," he emphasized.

"I had my parents' support for my actions and decisions throughout my life."

Ken remembered his father saying, "'When something is important to you, and you're involved in something that means a lot to you, whether people like you or not is not important.' That was instilled in me."

"I remember," reminisced Ken, "the first day at the University of Maryland, the very first day after registration. I was there and that was going to be my first night in a dorm. I felt strange. I walked around the campus in College Park, a beautiful campus. It was night. I sat on the steps of the chapel, which was on kind of a hill. As I gazed at university buildings and fraternity row, I had a real anxiety attack. 'Suppose I really don't learn anything here, don't get involved in anything, don't become successful,' In high school, I had been a 'Big Man on Campus'! This is large...it's like a city!"

CHAPTER THREE

Then Ken thought, "Yeah, well, but if in four years at the University of Maryland I accomplish nothing but studies, and don't become 'important' I'll take another crack at becoming important somewhere else.

"I suddenly relaxed, resigning myself to nothing happening for four years. I'll just have to live through it," thought Ken, "I'll make another opportunity that will put an end to the panic, an end to incredible impatience.'

"I was in the chorus of KISS ME KATE the second half of my first semester, that got me involved in my junior and senior years; I took a lot of theatre and journalism courses. I started drawing political cartoons for the campus newspaper; then I went to work on the Humor Magazine, eventually becoming Editor-in-Chief.

"I organized a vaudeville revue. Several years before, the University of Maryland had taken a theatre production to the Ozarks. It had been titled THE FLYING FOLLIES. The club we had formed adopted that name, but the show I put together was called FOOTLIGHT FEVER."

Did you get the club members together and say, 'Let's do this.'?

"It started that way," replied Ken. "We auditioned for specialty acts. One of the girl's mother wrote songs. She wrote a few original songs, including the title song, FOOTLIGHT FEVER. They were pretty good. A couple of the songs were great. I cast a very heavy girl to sing Chocolate Marshmallow Sundae, a novelty song. At the end she'd sing, 'leave the cherry off, I'm on a diet!'

"In our revue, I used two really beautiful girls, identical twins. I used them as mistresses of ceremony in the old vaudeville style of holding up a card to announce the next act. I kept it a secret from the audience that they were identical twins, and unless you knew them extremely well, you couldn't tell them apart. So the show began with a spotlight on the curtain, the curtain would open, and one twin would walk out and say, 'The University of Maryland's FLYING FOLLIES is delighted to be here tonight to present an original revue entitled, entitled...'

"She acted embarrassed, as if she couldn't remember her lines, and would feel for the center break of the curtain. A second after she had exited, from the other side of the stage the sister would enter saying, 'Oh yes, yes. A musical revue entitled FOOTLIGHTS, FOOTLIGHTS???' there she couldn't remember.

13

"She'd feel her way off with a kind of scared, fake laugh. The minute she was off, the other sister would appear from the other side.

"Audiences were puzzled as to how she got over there so fast,' " said Ken.

After a third entrance of a sister, the audiences would catch on and laugh.

"One of them having successfully delivered '...FOOTLIGHT FEVER,' the opening number would come on. Because it was unique and clever it went over everywhere.

"The twins also performed on stage together. This enabled us to create a particularly funny sketch. Two girls came out wearing the same outfits as the twins and holding cards introducing the next act over their faces. When they'd pull the cards down, it was not the twins. It was two girls wearing fright wigs and their teeth blacked out. Once again audiences were fooled. They loved it—audiences always do."

I asked Ken if he felt he may have been the 'prime mover.'

"I can see that I made it happen. All my accumulated experiences have served me on Broadway.

"On campus FOOTLIGHT FEVER was a great success. I had tried to get USO and Army people from Washington, DC, to come and see the show. They wouldn't. So I sent them a tape and an album of photos to let them know what the show was about. I used the university's public relations office for a mailing address.

"On April 1st, that office gave me a call, saying that a bureau in Washington had phoned me. (I was home in Baltimore, because it was over a holiday.) It was April 1st. The caller said, 'I just received a letter that the Army Professional Entertainment Bureau wants you to do a Caribbean tour of your show this summer.' I thought this was an April Fool joke. It was not. It was for real!

"When I got back to the campus, I started preparing the show. On campus I'd done FOOTLIGHT FEVER with 25 people. In the letter, playing a hunch, I had written that the show had a cast of 14 people. I had arbitrarily picked that number. When I saw the letter saying the Bureau wanted us to tour and it specified a cast of 14, I set about cutting the show. I picked the most versatile cast members; who could be backup chorus as well as perform solo spots.

CHAPTER THREE

Once again Ken was being challenged. Members of the Flying Follies Club told him, "The only fair way to decide who's going on this tour is to draw straws!"

"For the second time in my life—it was Junior Day assembly time all over again—I was being challenged by what I call the 'fairness doctrine,' which means to me, mediocrity."

Ken received a call from the Dean in charge of campus activities. The Dean ruled that Ken would have to arrive at a democratic solution.

Says Ken, "I showed the Dean the letter saying, 'The letter from the Special Entertainment Bureau is addressed to me. Personally! It refers to a show that I created; I put together. There was no reference to the University of Maryland. Therefore, we will do the tour as individuals. The University of Maryland will not be mentioned.'

"Well, now I get summoned to the university President's office. I had only seen the man in three years of college maybe four times. I walked in there and presented the same argument, even stronger, for I said to him, 'There's only one way to do a show. Democracy does not create shows. I decide who goes; I decide what they do; I decide where on the bill they are; I decide, because I'm the director.'"

Ken went on, "I produced FOOTLIGHT FEVER; I put it together. Now I am perfectly content to do it and not mention the name of the University of Maryland.

"Sure, if we get interviewed along the way and reporters ask us where we went to school, I guess, we'll say we go to the University of Maryland. But this will not be a University of Maryland show. That will solve the university's fairness problem."

As Ken savors telling it, the President of the University of Maryland said to him, "We're very proud to have the University of Maryland's name associated with FOOTLIGHT FEVER. We want it to be a touring show from the University of Maryland. So do what you want."

Ken relates another campus experience of his.

"As Editor-in-Chief of the campus HUMOR MAGAZINE I put out a 'sick' issue. It was a Valentine's Day issue, with a double cover, a trick cover. On the top cover was a typically fat girl, not attractive and with frizzy black hair. Like the ones one sees on contemporary cards. She was standing with her hands up in the middle of a heart and above her is a cupid aiming at her with an arrow. You turn the page;

it's the same cover, except she's lying flat dead with the arrow stuck in her.

"That spoof theme ran right through the whole issue. The issue did a takeoff on TRUE CONFESSIONS magazine. As one read the article, a girl was confessing to having started a bad habit. The so-called bad habit seemed to be sex, going to bed with guys, going 'all the way,' as they said then. The piece never actually said that, and at the very end, you find she's talking about cigarettes.

"The university administration treated drinking as a university today might treat cocaine or heroin. One beer found in a dorm room, and you could be expelled. We went to the university swimming pool, and we photographed an underwater beer party going on. The message: you have to hide out to have beer. The university really came down on me for that, also.

"The magazine was filled with ads. One was submitted for approval to the campus florist. I told them what kind of an issue we were putting out. The florist said, 'Okay, we'd like to run that ad.' It was of a person lying in a coffin, sitting up saying, 'I got my flowers from ...'

"The university went bananas. They threatened. They ordered me to stop publication, or they would kick me out of school. Not a word was to be mentioned to the press. They didn't want any news of the issue to get out.

"I immediately walked out of the meeting which to me was a kangaroo court. I telephoned the Baltimore Sun, the Baltimore News, the Washington Post, the Washington Star, the NBC news affiliate in Baltimore, the NBC news affiliate in Washington. All anonymously.

"Suddenly, the University of Maryland was on all the TV news programs. The word of the humorous Valentine's Day issue was in all the newspapers. Every one of the articles made the university look ridiculous. The magazine was out. What the university had done was to make the HUMOR MAGAZINE a collector's item.

"They could never prove I had sparked all the reporting. There were quotes from me, because once they came to the campus I did talk to them — which the university didn't like. One quote from me was, that I was not aware that the campus HUMOR MAGAZINE, paid for out of the students' activities fees, was a public relations vehicle for the university rather than for the students' enjoyment. That quote got everywhere.

CHAPTER THREE

"As editor I was to receive a stipend, a couple of thousand dollars. At the end of the year, the university refused to give it to me. The university was reneging because they didn't like that issue. So, again, I went to one of the newspapers in Baltimore. One of the columnists called the university and said he wanted to do a big story on the matter of the stipend. Within five days I had my check."

Ken concludes this part of his remembrance of things past as, "The need to be somebody in my college days life had been so important to me that I'd organized a show that a professional entertainment bureau in Washington had sent on tour, I had been Editor-in-Chief of the HUMOR MAGAZINE, and I had my own office in the journalism building. I was a campus celebrity."

CHAPTER FOUR

As Maxine sees it today, she went to an unusual high school in the suburbs of Baltimore.

I went to Forest Park High School. There the drama teacher taught plays like THE MADWOMAN OF CHAILLOT and a Czech drama, R. U. R. . She had an unusual, intelligent approach to theatre and drama for high school students. In high school my goal was acting, but I never seemed destined to be a performer.

"There were never any questions in my life. When high school kids go to see the school counselor about where they are going to college and what they're going to do, ninety-nine percent don't know what they want to be when they grow up. I knew from the time I was six; my meeting with the high school counselor was five minutes long; I knew to what school I wanted to apply and why. Boston University had a theatre program, and I could major in theatre in my Freshman year. I didn't want to wait for two years. I had taken dance classes until I was fourteen. But, it wasn't dancing anymore."

At Boston University Maxine was busy stage managing graduate directors' class scenes, and at the same time working in any capacity on all of the university's major productions.

"Acting didn't interest me; I wanted production experience. I got valuable experience in Boston's theatres; e.g. the Charles Playhouse; stage managing, building scenery. I found I'd get a 'rush' helping to put a production together, seeing it happen.

The summer after Maxine's freshman year in college, she worked at the Painters Mill Music Fair (a summer theatre) doing props, running up and down the aisles dressed in black, supervising the apprentices. Apparently, the producers liked the work she was doing, for one day, Lee Guber and Shelly Gross were in Baltimore to look at one of their shows.

"They asked me to come to New York to work for them in the fall! I was thunderstruck; I was eighteen years old. I had an offer to work in a producer's office in Manhattan. I had a decision to make; either go back to college and finish my education or come to New York.

Was there any fear about moving to New York?

"No, there never was any question from the time that I was very young that I would live in the city, work there, and work there in theatre. It was only a question of when."

Maxine's mother and father came up to New York with her. They had heard about a place called the Rehearsal Club on West 53rd street, near the Museum of Modern Art. It was a residence for young women who were in the performing arts. Maxine and her parents checked it out, and that's where she stayed.

"I was fortunate when I came to New York. I knew at least four hundred people from summer shows. I had moved into a residence club where I was not alone. I had a roof over my head, and I had a job."

Just like the movie STAGE DOOR, the girls at the Rehearsal Club were teenagers to young women in their mid-twenties. Everybody was either studying or performing. Most were studying and looking for work. Maxine was one of the few people working in a non-performing aspect of theatre. The Club didn't know that much about what she was doing, because she really should have been seeking acting jobs.

Recalling her stay at the Rehearsal Club, Maxine had this to say, "We had our meals there, and it cost me $23.00 for room and three meals a day! It was, truly, reasonable. My salary check from my job was $33.00 a week. I had ten bucks to blow each week! The club did have house rules; no men above the first floor. It wasn't strict, however, not as strict as a college dormitory."

Maxine began working for a producing organization that sent out 'bus and truck' tours. While she was working for them, the company sent out a tour of the Broadway musical CARNIVAL. It was a very exciting experience for Maxine.

"I handled the office end of it, some rehearsal assignments. When it went out of town to open, I went with it as the production assistant.

CHAPTER FOUR

"Here I was in my late teens sitting between a director and choreographer; at the same time taking their notes, and giving actors the director's notes on their performances.

Maxine stayed with Guber and Gross for two years, then they were cutting back on office staff, and they said that she should look for something else to do. Maxine sent letters to a lot of theatre people. One of the letters was sent to writer-director-producer Garson Kanin, because she knew he was preparing to direct a new musical titled FUNNY GIRL starring Barbra Streisand. Mr. Kanin called her in for an interview.

"We hit it off. He gave me a job as receptionist in his office! But I was also assigned to do research for the show. Perfectly fine for me. Just being around a Broadway show at this time was a big step up for me. I did nearly everything, I even learned to work their incredible switchboard."

Maxine does not dismiss any way of gaining entrance into the Broadway theatre. Her advice is, "If you can take shorthand and type and that gets you a job in a producer's office, the job puts you in a place where you can ask questions. Then you're a step ahead of the game. "As I see it," adds Maxine, "it's just a matter of being around, and that's real important!"

It never occurred to her to say to a prospective employer, "I'm not a secretary." She admits to a truth that she's a lousy secretary.

"My secretarial skills were not great, but my skill was that I could anticipate the boss's needs. More important than being able to file or type a letter expertly."

When Maxine started working with Garson Kanin, he told her that any free time she had, she could come to rehearsal.

"Every lunch hour, every minute I was away from the office, I'd be observing the rehearsal, and I was available to do anything. Running for coffee, making helpful telephone calls; I was prepared to do anything to be around where the show was being done."

One day, Maxine bumped into Barbra Streisand who was on her way to composer Jule Styne's office. His office was in the same building as Garson Kanin's. Jule Styne was late; Streisand had to wait for him. Maxine said, "Listen, Miss Streisand, while you're waiting, do you want to go over your lines?"

Barbra Streisand replied, "Sure, I'd love to."

So there they were; Maxine Fox and Barbra Streisand sitting in the lobby of an office building going over pages of Barbra Streisand's new lines for FUNNY GIRL.

"It started a whole new rhythm that we got into; if Barbra had some free time, she'd send for me. Mr. Kanin allowed me to come down to rehearsal, run lines with Barbra. Then, I'd go back to the office when she'd go on rehearsing.

"We got to the point where we had a lot of fun with with it. We got comfortable with each other."

Maxine wasn't to go out of town with FUNNY GIRL; Garson Kanin's personal secretary was going to work with him during out-of-town tryouts of the show.

"Barbra asked me if I'd come to work for her. Her career was just beginning to take off, and she realized she needed a personal secretary."

Maxine replied, "Well, I can't leave Mr. Kanin in the middle of a production. Let me think about it. I'll let you know in Boston when the show opens up there."

Maxine thought about it and decided she was going to do it.

"I decided I'd tell Mr. Kanin that I was leaving him to work for Barbra Streisand, after the show opened in New York."

CHAPTER FIVE

When Ken was in college he would say, "I'm going to New York."

Friends would come back with, "Oh, you got to be in the 'right' place at the 'right' time. Forget it! It's a one in a two million, three million shot."

Ken's answer was, "Well, you know if you're in the right place long enough, you'll be there at the right time."

Ken now believes, "Persistence is the key to success!"

Ken went to New York University's Graduate School for training in television, film and theatre. [He attended classes in 1963-64.]

"When I was in school taking courses in theatre, films and television, I was upset that nowhere was there any nitty-gritty training in these areas; not even was there discussion that would be of a pragmatic nature. I attended Graduate School at New York University, The School of the Arts, which is now called The Tisch School of the Arts, and the other students and I used to raise questions. The answer given was, 'We're studying the arts here. If you're asking about getting a job, this is an educational institution. We don't train for a vocation. We're above that."

Ken's answer was, "My parents, who are footing the bill, are not above that. They want to know what a son or daughter does after one learns to be an actor, or director, or writer, or producer."

Ken was frustrated that there never were any courses on how to get an audition, what to do at an audition; how to survive in New York while you are waiting for interviews.

"What alternatives are there in the entertainment business if you decide that acting, or directing, is not for you?

"If you are a performer, how do you deal with agents; what is an agent? How does one get any practical theatre experience?"

Ken wanted to be taught the many pragmatic things that have nothing to do with how an actor develops a character or how a writer write a script. He felt getting a job has everything to do with education if you're going to make the theatre your life work.

"As a kid, I'd found out that the producer was the boss. I wanted to be the boss. So that was going to be my thing."

Little did Ken realize that he would be deflected from his goal to make it to Broadway as a 'boss,' a producer of shows.

Sergeant Shriver of the Peace Corps came and talked to the graduate students. He spoke of the special projects in Bogotá, Colombia, South America. The country of Colombia had a national television network with cultural and educational programs. Ken's interest was aroused. Ken was selected, because he had had practical experience and had worked in theatre.

"I did it partly for the adventure of it; partly because I was caught up in the mystique of the Kennedy administration. I admit, too, I wanted to avoid the draft, because I could see a draft call coming quickly. I was the right age. As long as I had been in school, I was pretty safe."

Having the opportunity to learn a foreign language, to be able to speak it while living in a foreign country, and to work in a different culture appealed to Ken. He hoped he would be able to do things in Colombia that he would not be able to do in the States for many years: to produce television shows, to work with people older than himself, and all in another language. He had been told that he would be working with co-workers who spoke no English.

Ken now believes that, "Staying power is probably one of the biggest keys to success."

To get the work done, to get the programs on despite cultural barriers was more frustrating, Ken found out, than he'd anticipated.

The Peace Corps training gave him a basic command of Spanish. Ken says, "I had had instruction in the language for five hours a day for three months, but I felt I could hardly say a thing in Spanish. I did not understand anything. I guess , however, I knew more Spanish than I realized. Once in Bogotá, I started catching on real fast. When you have to use a language, that's when you learn it!"

In Bogotá, Colombia, he worked for the national television network and developed a series of musical programs.

CHAPTER FIVE

"In some ways, our LA CASA DE MUSICA (MUSIC HOUSE) was almost like a forerunner of SESAME STREET.

"Amalia Samper, a charming woman, a musicologist I worked with, had studied in the States and had studied in Europe. "She was really lovely," remembers Ken. "She was from the 'aristocracy,' which looked upon her as a renegade. To be involved in the Peace Corps and in social programs for underprivileged children made her somewhat of a black sheep, a 'hippie.' She was about as 'hippie' as Nancy Reagan!

"The programs were done as fairy tales. Amalia as a 'Shirley Temple' character with apron opened the fairy tale house. There were two hand puppets; one a burro, one a cow.

"The burro would visit at the window with Rosa, the cow. Rosa always spoke correctly and knew everything and learned everything. The burro always made mistakes; he was the comic character.

"Our goal was to teach children: to teach them music; to teach them to think; to teach them to express themselves. We would ask them to 'draw' the lyrics to the song. That's how they learned the lyrics. We wanted them to learn to use their imaginations."

LA CASA DE MUSICA showed them how to make musical instruments simply: drums, triangles, gourd-type rattles. They were instructed how to make them out of bottles, pieces of wood, gourd, or any scraps. The hostess and the puppets would play the drum, the triangle and other instruments; the children viewing the television screen were urged to play along with rhythm sticks.

"Everybody had to come in at the right time. We were teaching them singing, too. We had a magic piano. It was a prop piano, but it played magically. We used tapes of piano music. Our hostess, Amalia, would play a Columbian instrument which sounded like a guitar and was the size of a guitar. But, it was strung like a ukulele, and each of the four strings were doubled strings. An unusual, indigenous instrument."

In addition to LA CASA DE MUSICA, the network produced educational programs. Programs on the social sciences, history, mathematics, health, and programs to combat illiteracy. The programs were transmitted by the network throughout the country.

"The Ford Foundation and the Phillips Company had given television sets to schools, churches, and social halls. In all the schools the children could watch a television set. Peace Corps volunteers traveled to different towns, big and little, and went into the schools and showed the teachers how to turn on the sets! They worked hard to arouse the interest, to motivate the teachers to use the educational programs in their classes. Schools were given manuals and text books that could be used along with the programs. They were given guides to follow up the activities on the television for discussions with the school children.

"The country of Colombia has about six major cities. Many homes in the cities have television, for there is a large middle class in each of the cities. The population of Bogotá is about 2,500,000 people. Seven hundred and fifty to eight hundred thousand are middle class and have one or more television sets.

"But the Peace Corps' real goal was to teach the hinterland. The population of Colombia is about 23,000,000; out of the total population, the majority are poor. Eighteen million people are living in the 'Dark Ages,' living in primitive towns. Most are illiterate, although school is mandatory. Kids may go to school through the eighth grade, but they learn by rote. A minimum of reading, a minimum of math, a minimum of history — and only by rote. They are not encouraged to express themselves.

"Here we are producing programs to get the kids to think and express themselves! And, we were doing it with local government cooperation. However, as the government began to realize just exactly what we were doing, it got harder and harder to get their cooperation."

One of the things Ken hoped they'd do was to verify the popularity of LA CASA DE MUSICA, so the Colombian government would have to continue the program.

"A staff from Stanford University was sent to Bogotá to poll responses to different programs. What their responses were; how popular they were; how many people were watching. The government of Colombia was anxious to have the Peace Corps, and a recommendation from the Stanford University staff could encourage the government of Colombia to cooperate. We were certain they were not going to ignore the facts!"

LA CASA DE MUSICA had been on the air once a week, then twice a week, and then three times a week. During the two years, 1965-66, that Ken was in Colombia, he taped the Monday, Tuesday, and Wednesday programs in the studio in Bogotá. To promote the programs every other week or so, Thursday, Friday, and Saturday, the

CHAPTER FIVE

cast and crew would go out into the field to put on a live version of the show in a town.

"We traveled hours on mud roads to remote little towns. We did this to build audiences for the show on television, to promote it. We'd take along the puppets, and a part of the set which we'd fold up and get onto a truck or a plane. The show was an enormous success in places we went."

Small wonder to me that later Ken's and Maxine's producing organization would tour GREASE; widely and frequently throughout the USA and abroad.

"We did the live shows of LA CASA DE MUSICA in theatres, movie houses, churches, halls, any gathering place. Whatever we could find.

"As a price of admission, the kids had to bring one of the instruments that we had shown them how to make on television.

"One little girl walked in one day; she couldn't have been more than five years old; she carried a drum with daisies, roses and lace around it. Obviously, she hadn't made it, but she was clutching her drum as her ticket of admission. There was always a prize; she won the prize. As the shy, five-year-old got up on stage with her drum, she said with poise,'Thank you, my mother helped me and we were up all night.'

"When the kids went home and would try to explain to their parents what television was, the parents often didn't understand. Even the kids weren't quite sure what they were watching, either."

Ken would introduce the show, "You know who you are going to see today?" And the kids would yell, "La Señorita Amalia!"

"That's right. She's here and you're going to see her today."

As he was talking, La Señorita Amalia would start playing her guitar offstage. All eyes would move to the wings and the hostess would walk on-stage.

"The kids were in total shock. Even when they'd answered my question as to whom they were going to see, they didn't know she was going to be there in the flesh.

"Until that moment the kids had never understood that what they had seen on a television screen was a real person of flesh and blood. However, we realized that Hollywood didn't invent the 'star' idea. They only capitalized on a phenomenon of human nature.

"The second they realized she was real, they behaved as if they were fans of the Beatles. Screaming, they had to touch and clutch. We learned from our first trips to the villages that we had to have plenty of security for all of us all the time.

"On one of these trips, the whole live presentation had been given in a big movie palace. Kids had come in from schools all over. There must have been 2,000 of them.

"Later all the props had been stacked in the Jeep, and I was checking to see if everything was back. A little kid about six years old was peeking in the Jeep, looking all around. I said, 'What are you looking for?' He said, 'I'm looking for Pasqual.' Pasqual was the donkey on the show.

"'Oh!' I said, 'Pasqual is not here. He had to go back to Bogotá. He took a train back; he's gone.'

"The child started to cry. I saw he was clutching something behind his back. I said, 'What's the matter?'

"'Well,' he said, 'I stayed up real late last night to make Pasqual a gift. I couldn't get close enough to him today in all the mob to give it to him.' He held up a hat that we had shown them how to make on television. It was made just the way we had shown them, except that he had added his own touches. Two holes for Pasqual's ears and a ribbon for Pasqual to hold it on with. He'd written on the hat, 'I love you, Pasqual,' and had signed his name. It was really quite remarkable. He'd printed his school, his town and his provincial department. Very unusual, because most hadn't known what country they were living in, until they started watching television. They'd never been to a town. The fact that he had been able to write was truly impressive."

Moved, Ken replies, "Listen, I'm going to see Pasqual as soon as I get back. If you want to give me the hat, I'll see that he gets it. You keep watching LA CASA DE MUSICA. He'll wear your hat on the television program."

When Ken got back, he wrote it into the script, and a week or so later, Pasqual appeared on television wearing the child's hat.

The hostess asked, "Pasqual, where did you get that lovely hat?"

The puppet, Pasqual replied, "This is a gift from a very good friend of mine." Pasqual mentioned the little boy's name, his school and town; adding, "He made it especially for me. He's my friend."

A week later, there was a reception at the American Embassy in Bogota for new Peace Corps volunteers who had been working in an

CHAPTER FIVE

agricultural development project. They had been in the area where the kid lived who had made the hat for Pasqual. When Ken walked in, one of the Peace Corps men walked over to him and said, "I don't know what you did, but there's a kid who's the hero of the town. They were carrying him around on their shoulders because he was mentioned on national television."

Ken says, "That gave me a lot of satisfaction. LA CASA DE MUSICA had been on the air once a week, then twice a week, and then three times a week. When I left Bogotá, it was on four times a week. I had trained the hostess to take over as producer, and I had trained a bright fellow to take over as director. The program continued to play for a while after I left. Later, bureaucratic interference prompted the hostess, Amalia, to decide that she no longer wanted to do LA CASA DE MUSICA. For a time, they reran shows I had done. As far as I know, they are still rerunning old programs."

Ken reminisced, "GREASE has played all over the United States and in many parts of the world. Because of my experience producing in Colombia, my having acquired a command of the Spanish language (which I keep up by watching Spanish programs on television), I especially enjoyed seeing the the production of GREASE (called VASALINA) in Mexico. It ran for 2 years, becoming at that time the longest run musical in Mexico City.

"Mexican audiences appreciated the musical numbers, but the book they took very seriously. American audiences had found the end of the first act amusing: they had laughed at the heroine Sandy's being so upset as she says to her boyfriend Zuko, 'You don't really like me, and I don't want to see you anymore.' She runs off. Mexican audiences were practically in tears. They had been taking it literally. Latin audiences' reactions differ greatly.

"For Mexico the producers had changed the jokes that were particularly American. And, of course they changed the bit about 'Mooning.' They completely changed it. First of all, they didn't understand it. And, secondly, under their censorship it was too risqué. When the tune for 'Mooning" came up, although I fully understood the Spanish of the lyrics, I didn't understand why the whole house got hysterical. They were howling with laughter.

"Backstage, it was explained to us. In Mexico City dial 0-5 for information. No one evidently ever gets through to information. The call is a whole waste of time. In the lyrics, in substitution for the song of a 'Mooning Champion,' the Mexican counterpart sings, 'You know, I'm the expert on 0-5!'

"It worked for their audiences, and we got the feeling seeing the Mexican production that these were Mexican kids in a Mexican high school."

"After the opening-night performance, Maxine and I went backstage to meet the actors. In Spanish, I gave them compliments. One of the actors asked if we thought they were good enough to play GREASE on Broadway. I said,'perhaps. How many of you speak English?' With that, there was silence. Finally, one member of the company said,'We never thought of that!' "

CHAPTER SIX

At the time FUNNY GIRL was taking place, Bob Merrill, who wrote the lyrics, would call the office and say to Maxine, "I need a description of a car of the period," or, "I need a list of products in use in the period of FUNNY GIRL." She'd do all that without leaving the office.

Maxine was very resourceful. She didn't want to go to the public library every day. So she found a way of doing research by telephone. For example, she'd call up CAR AND DRIVER magazine and say, "Listen, I really need to know what kind of cars there were in 1920. What makes of cars were around at the time?" She telephoned the experts. If she needed to know what a roller skate of the period looked like, she'd call Sears and Roebuck and put the question to one of the persons who put the Sears catalogue together. He was able and agreeable to go back into the files and describe skates that were in the catalogue for any of the years of FUNNY GIRL."

Isobel Lennart told her that she functioned five times faster than the entire Research Department at 20th Century Fox.

For FUNNY GIRL, Maxine went up to Boston on weekends on her own money; she wanted to be where it was happening.

Opening night in Boston, FUNNY GIRL ran four hours long, because Mr. Kanin, as director, had wanted to see all the show onstage before he would cut it. The show played from 8:30 p.m. until 12:30 a.m. After the show, Mr. Kanin and the writers slashed whole scenes, eliminated sets, and eliminated most of the lines for one character. This heightened the anxieties of the producers. After opening night, Kanin kept editing until FUNNY GIRL ran two hours and twenty minutes.

Maxine returned to New York. The show moved to Philadelphia. Maxine got a call at the office from Garson Kanin telling her that he was sending his personal secretary back to New York, and he wanted her to come down to Philadelphia. "I was really excited," as Maxine expressed it. "Wow! I had my chance to work on the show, to be out of town with it. I was all excited. This was my first Broadway show."

Maxine took the train to Philadelphia. "I walked into the theatre for the rehearsal. The production secretary, who worked with the authors as well as with Mr. Kanin, said to me, 'What are you doing here? Look, I can't be seen talking to you. Meet me around the corner for dinner.' She walked away."

Maxine had been puzzled as to why Garson Kanin's personal secretary, Marian, had been sent back to New York, but now she was really surprised. Over dinner with the production secretary, she learned that the show had broken down into two factions, with Garson Kanin, as director, on one side; Barbra Streisand, as star, on the other. "Barbra didn't feel she was getting enough from the director; she'd called her acting coach to help her. Marian had been sent back to New York, because she had been seen talking with Barbra's acting coach. What a situation for me," thought Maxine.

"I learned much from that painful experience, as I did later from two hits and a flop which followed. I felt I was getting to know how Broadway works and how to cope with it. So often two factions become pitted against each other."

I, too, heard from George Eells that Garson Kanin had found his involvement in FUNNY GIRL the most destructive experience in his life. So many like Kanin give up directing musicals because of production by committee!

The whole company of FUNNY GIRL was on stage, ready to rehearse. Ray Stark, the producer of FUNNY GIRL, walked down the aisle with Jerome Robbins. He turned to the company and said, "Ladies and Gentlemen, I would like you to meet your new director, Jerome Robbins."

Maxine turned to the production supervisor and said, "What do I do now, David? I'd better call Mr. Kanin and find out what he wants me to do."

Kanin told Maxine to remain at rehearsal and find out what Jerome Robbins was doing. But after that day, she was not allowed into the theatre. She had been branded a spy. She was able to go to performances.

CHAPTER SIX

"I was frustrated, and I was in agony. Each day, I took dictation from Mr. Kanin; I brought letters back to my hotel room; I typed them; I got the letters signed.

"Garson Kanin stayed in Philadelphia throughout the whole rumpus. He'd been locked out of the theatre. His lawyers had advised him to stay in Philadelphia. I thought about it and thought about it. I soon realized I couldn't handle this. I wanted to be part of a Broadway show, but I was only being a secretary and had no contact with the show (by now they'd barred me from performances, too!). I had to leave, even if it meant burning my bridges. I was too young to deal with the pulls and tugs on me."

She told Garson Kanin she had to leave. She told Barbra Streisand she'd be in New York when FUNNY GIRL opened; and would start working with her right after the opening.

"That's exactly what happened. It was a terrible thing for me to go through, knowing that I was about to 'shaft' Mr. Kanin when everybody else had. But I had to do it.

"When my father came to pick me up, I insisted that he pay the hotel bill. My boss, Mr. Kanin, had been paying my hotel bill, and it was the only thing I could think of to relieve some of the guilt I was feeling."

Maxine did come back to New York and began working for Barbra Streisand. That was another kind of experience. "I saw her at a time when she was part 'insecure little girl,' part 'super star.' FUNNY GIRL had sent her over the top to stardom. She was making the PEOPLE album. She was feeling the 'rush' of everything happening to her and at the same time not up to dealing with it. This was the first time I'd ever worked for anyone on a personal level."

Because of Barbra Streisand, Maxine was kicked out of the Rehearsal Club. While she was working for Streisand, she decided that she should have her own phone. If Barbra called, she'd get the Rehearsal Club, not Maxine. Maxine applied for a telephone on her own which was unheard of at the Rehearsal Club. In examining the request, the Doyenne of the residence club realized that she wasn't a performer, and wasn't going to acting classes.

Miss Streisand had a maid's room in her New York apartment converted into an office. Maxine worked there.

In addition to Maxine's own problem of where to live as a single, young girl in New York, she had to solve the problem of getting

MAKING A BROADWAY MUSICAL

Barbra Streisand in FUNNY GIRL

CHAPTER SIX

Barbra Streisand out of the theatre after her performances in FUNNY GIRL at the Winter Garden. Wednesday and Saturday matinees and each night, there were mobs of fans at the stage door. Barbra Streisand was afraid of her fans and people in general. Maxine would gather all the programs from the fans and the crowds waiting outside the theatre. They wanted Streisand's autograph.

"Actually," sighed Maxine, "I ended up signing them in a dressing room backstage, and the doorman would distribute them. Barbra's handwriting and mine are similar, and I had learned how to write her name. If Barbra Streisand had acceded to all the demands of her fans, she'd have had little energy left for performing and her recording sessions," reasoned Maxine.

For six months, Maxine was fascinated with being personal secretary to Barbra Streisand. She would show up at the end of the performance of FUNNY GIRL every night. "Barbra had a two-room dressing room, one was a living room area, the inner room was the mirrored dressing room. I'd play hostess in Streisand's dressing room to friends and celebrities who came backstage.

"I met a lot of terrific people that way. One night, there was a knock at the door. I opened the door, and there was this short man standing there. He said, 'We've never met, but my name is Frank Sinatra. I wonder if Miss Streisand would see me.' I said, playing it cool, 'Sure, come on in.'

"I often laugh over the night that Elizabeth Taylor and Richard Burton came to see FUNNY GIRL and came backstage. I'm not much of a drinker, and I'm no bartender. But one of the things I had to do for Barbra's guests was to fix drinks. The Burtons were in the dressing room and were waiting for Barbra. Each wanted vodka on the rocks. I had heard stories about Burton's and Peter O'Toole's drinking bouts during the filming of BECKET. I poured Burton the stiffest drink he'd probably ever had (I thought!). Burton's drink was okay for him. Elizabeth Taylor, I think, was amused, but she wanted me to make hers less potent.

"The challenge remained always for me to get Barbra out of the theatre. If we had the car pick her up in front of the theatre, the fans caught on to that very quickly. They'd end up racing around in front of the theatre. We tried different things almost every night for Barbra.

"Some people carry being a star better than others. Barbra Streisand felt she did her job by performing and giving of her talent.

But, once it was over, she didn't feel the responsibility went beyond that. In a way, I quarrel with that.

"During this period, the film people had not begun to take an interest in Barbra, but she was forming her own company. I was really involved in all aspects of her life at that point. She was still married to Elliot Gould.

"I was becoming frustrated. There was not enough action for me. When you work for a star, as I did, you don't participate in show business, which is all around you. You participate in the star's life. I felt left out of all that was going on in the theatre. Moreover, I wasn't right for the job; I was too young to be a personal secretary to a young superstar. Someone more experienced should have that job.

"She was real comfortable with me, though, and it was the whole romance of two young girls learning the ins and outs of show business. For six months I was just learning as I went along. So was Barbra. I learned a whole lot, and I've used the knowledge in dealing with stars. I'm never intimidated by them, ever. Dealing with a celebrity is easy for me, because I know how to make them comfortable.

"Barbra and I sat down one day, and we agreed to go our separate ways. There were no ill feelings."

Maxine was unemployed, but only briefly. She sent out letters again and was interviewed by people for whom she really wanted to work. She does not remember a whole lot about the interviews except the one with Sylvia Harris of Fryer, Carr, and Harris.

"Sylvia Harris asked me, 'Why do you want to work for us?' My answer was, 'Because I respect the work that you've done.' That one statement got me the job. They fired the receptionist to make a place for me. From there I was in a position to watch rehearsals of SWEET CHARITY.

"I found it fascinating, because the musical had started out as two one-act musicals. Bob Fosse and Elaine May had been the writers. Elaine May dropped out. Midstream, the producers took the first one-act, which was Bob Fosse's, and expanded it into a two-act musical. Watching Fosse work was great for me.

"SWEET CHARITY reopened the Palace Theatre as a theatre. After being vaudeville's flagship, it had deteriorated as movie house. It was a very exciting opening.

"One of the most valuable things that happened to me from my work on SWEET CHARITY was meeting Betty Lee Hunt, a press

CHAPTER SIX

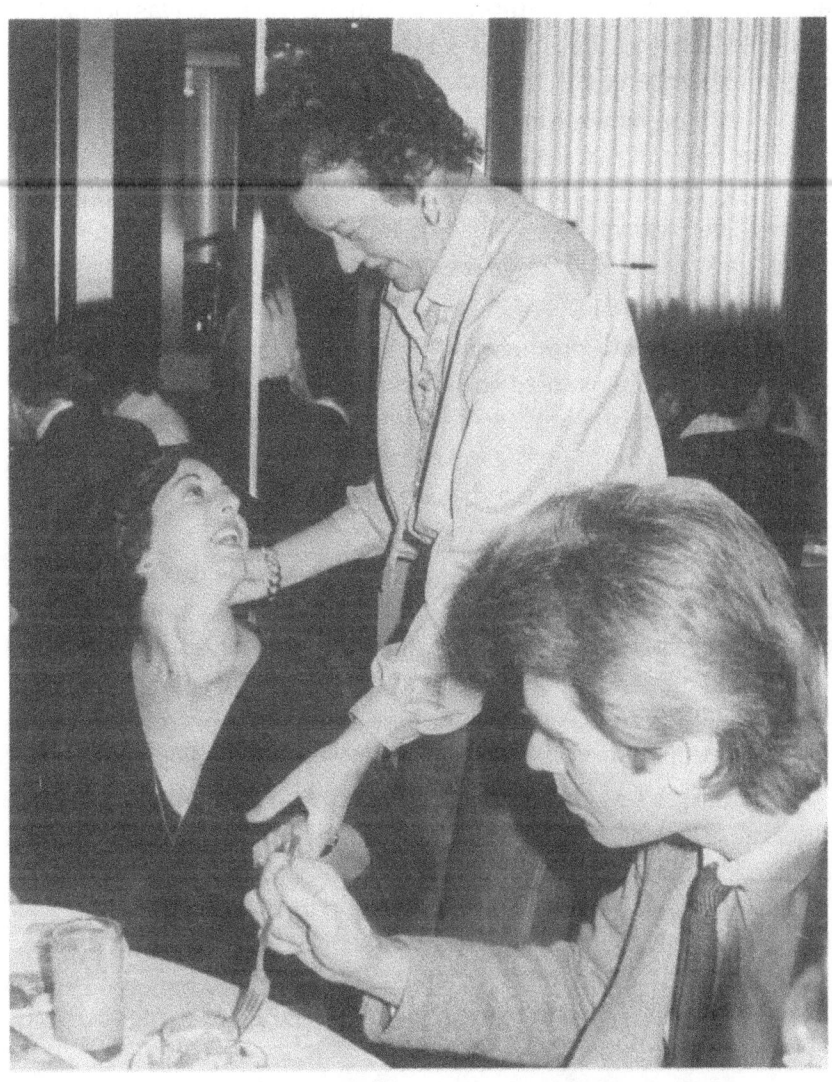

Maxine Fox, Betty Lee Hunt (Press Agent) & Barry Bostwick

agent. I remember being impressed with the work she was doing. For example, she had the SWEET CHARITY logo printed on shopping bags. I remembered her for that.

"Later on, when Ken and I formed our partnership and he was flipping through my SWEET CHARITY scrapbooks, he kept asking me, 'Who got this in the papers?' and, 'Who got that in the papers?.' The answer was always Betty Lee Hunt." Betty Lee had been with Fryer, Carr, and Harris for years.

Sometime after SWEET CHARITY opened, Fryer, Carr and Harris put MAME into production. As the time got closer and closer to rehearsals, Maxine wanted to go on that show. The office tried their best to keep her as executive secretary. The assistant to the producers kept saying, "You're giving up steady employment." Maxine said, "Yeah, I know I am taking a risk, but I really have to take it. And, I'm willing to take it."

The director, Gene Saks, agreed to let Maxine work with him. She left the office and went on to work on the production of MAME. She was giving up security, for after the show had opened there would be no guarantee that she would have a job. Maxine looks back on it as a 'fabulous experience' for her: sitting with the director, taking his notes, seeing the show through his eyes, watching it grow.

"This was Angela Lansbury's first starring role on Broadway in a musical. They had considered everybody to get the right Mame. Patrice Munsel waged a campaign to get the job, for it was a prize role. They decided on Angela. The big question in everybody's mind was: did Angela have the voice? They worked on her voice, and decided she could do it. I remember when Angela Lansbury saw the posters for the first time. She had tears in her eyes seeing her name above the title of a musical.

"Since MAME I've heard that Angela can be very difficult. I'm convinced that it must have to do with her sometimes not feeling secure. No trouble in MAME: she was in excellent hands. The director was very strong; the producers knew their show and were very strong. She could trust them. There proved to be very few problems with Angela.

"I was able to observe what happens when a cast is in the strong hands of seasoned producers, as opposed to producers who are shaky and insecure. They don't trust anyone. MAME was one of the highlights of my early career."

CHAPTER SIX

Maxine's work was very different from that of the stage manager. She was out front all the time working with the director and the authors. She would prepare script changes; make sure they got to the cast; she would take the director's notes during the performance and give them to him for the next day's rehearsal. Or, later that night she'd follow the director from dressing room to dressing room as he gave actors notes.

"I had typed the notes. I didn't type fast, but they were totally accurate and neat. I have some skills. I went to a speed writing school on 42nd Street when I first got to town. I use it to this day when I'm on the phone and somebody is talking very fast.

"I also ran for coffee; got Gene cigarettes when he needed them. I made myself helpful. I realized anyone in my role of assisting a director is there to give service. You can' indulge your ego and you're gonna get 'beat on.' They dare not take it out on the actors; they can't take it out on the stagehands. It was part of my job, and I understood that. I had to be selfless.

"I didn't realize then how much I had absorbed while I was working on both shows until I actually had to use the knowledge in producing GREASE. My focus had been on the production: getting the feeling of an out-of-town shape up.

"After the opening of MAME there was nothing else for me to do. The show had opened, and that was that. I was unemployed. That was 1966."

Maxine had worked on three Broadway hits up to that point: FUNNY GIRL, SWEET CHARITY, and MAME. She started working on a show called A JOYFUL NOISE in the summer of 1966. It was on the summer stock circuit in theatres-in-the round and was coming to Broadway. It was also Michael Bennet's first Broadway musical as a choreographer and one of the featured dancers was Tommy Tune. She was hired to cast the show. She now finds it surprising that she had been hired to do all the casting.

"I didn't approach it from any point of view. I just set up auditions. They say, 'A truly good casting director is creative.' I suppose I got away with murder, but they were paying me next to nothing to get a cast for the show. I sent out cast lists to the agents, and I got their suggestions. I fear I wasn't creative about it at all, but I did the casting. Looking back, it strikes me as funny."

Maxine worked in the producers' office, setting up the show. Once the show went into rehearsal, she became Dore Schary's assistant, and assistant stage manager.

This was the first big musical Maxine worked on that was not successful. "When we got into previews, the show was in trouble. It wasn't happening. Dore Schary was making the revisions on the book as well as directing. It wasn't coming together. One day, in a very brutal way, one of the producers fired him. He took over the show himself. The way it was done was very ugly.

"I had been working with Mr. Schary on revisions. He would call me at home at night, give me the changes over the phone. I would type them up, bring them into rehearsal the next day.

"I'll never forget the first time I had to type up the new director's revisions. After working with a wise and wonderful man like Mr. Schary I could barely get myself to type them up. I hated any kind of contact with him, but I did what I had agreed to do. A JOYFUL NOISE opened and closed. Once again, I was unemployed.

"Arthur Whitelaw was producing a Broadway show. He'd been talking to my father about investing. I met him, and he asked me to be associate producer. I think I got the job, because he was interested in getting my father to invest.

"While we were trying to get the Broadway show into production, Whitelaw came across an off-Broadway property that he wanted to produce. He said to me, 'Look, while we're getting this other thing together, would you consider being my assistant and casting director for the off-Broadway show that I want to do?' I said, 'Sure.' "

The Broadway show never happened. The off-Broadway project was YOU'RE A GOOD MAN, CHARLIE BROWN.

"I cast it from the beginning."

Maxine, as yet, had not met Ken.

"It's strange because Ken's family and mine had been members of the same country club. We could have met, but we hadn't."

CHARLIE BROWN opened in March of 1967, and it was a hit.

"I met Ken in August of 1967, and we started dating right in the middle of the run of CHARLIE BROWN."

Maxine was busy with the others in setting up other companies. CHARLIE BROWN was the first off-Broadway show to set up sit-down companies in other places across the United States. There were companies in San Francisco, Los Angeles, and Boston. She cast the Toronto company.

"Since I helped form the Company for Toronto, Whitelaw asked me to go up there and manage it. I'd never done that before.

"Ken and I were on the phone a lot. There I was in Toronto, Canada, in the dead of winter managing a company and managing a theatre. It was another new experience. I'd worked props; I had worked for producers; worked for directors; worked for a a star; had been a stage manager and now, I was a company and theatre manager.

"Finally, after a year with CHARLIE BROWN, I got really tired of six people on a little stage doing little things. It got to me. I was not making a lot of money. It just seemed to me that there was an inequity here. I was doing all this work. I asked the producer for a raise.

"I was turned down. The manager who replaced me was a man; he was given a salary twice what I was making. I knew my decision had been the right one. I'd put a great deal of myself into that show."

I asked Maxine if she was a feminist.

"No. Those of us who are professional women in the theatre would have done what we're doing whether the business world were male oriented or not. Some women buy in at the top, but those of us who came up through the ranks would have arrived in any event."

I cited for Maxine that a character in a recent novel I had read says, "It really isn't a question of equal rights, it's being able to take equal responsibility. Because being male or female isn't important. It's that you've got what it takes and can deliver." I asked Maxine what she thought of that.

"The way I was programmed as a child, I never came to feel that I was a woman in business. I was a person doing a job: being a woman didn't affect what I did. I have spent many an hour in meetings, the only woman among men. I have never felt any less respect from them being a woman.

"In gut level business, a woman with a good head has to be better than her male counterpart to gain equal recognition. Women have been dealing with this for years."

CHAPTER SEVEN

Ken returned from his South American Peace Corps stint in the fall of 1966. After a brief speaking tour of various universities, he arrived back in New York "to do the rest of my life," as he recalls. A former NYU cohort, Sona Robbins, was producing an interview show for Channel 13, New York's PBS (public broadcasting station) channel. She arranged a 'test' for Ken as program host; he was hired.

"It was a 12-week series and the pay was extremely good," Ken remembers. "Actually, this was an exciting and glamorous experience - being on television and being able to save a nest egg of money which would come in handy later! But my youthful impatience took over and I felt trapped in a forever-like situation. What did this have to do with Broadway producing? I diligently wrote to Broadway producers for work, but to no avail."

Following the series Ken landed a job as production assistant for the CBS soap operas SECRET STORM and LOVE OF LIFE.

"There I was, taking notes for the director, timing scenes with a stop watch, booking actors...not bad for a 'showbiz' beginning."

However, once again impatience set in. "Poor me," Ken continues, "look where I am...and my high school friend, Ellen Cohen's voice is blearing out of every radio in the nation as Cass Elliot of the Mamas and Papas!"

When Ken met Maxine, he had just begun working for veteran producer/director George Abbott. He read that 'Mr. Abbott,' as his colleagues refer to him, was doing a new musical entitled THE EDUCATION OF HYMAN KAPLAN. "I wrote his office," says Ken.

"When I received no response I took my resumé, cut it down the middle with a pinking shears and attached a note which read: if you wish to see the other half of me, I'm available at your convenience."

Waissman was given a job. He worked for Mr. Abbott on two shows; HYMAN KAPLAN and THE FIG LEAVES ARE FALLING. Although both shows folded shortly after opening Ken had studied under the master. "A priceless experience!" says Ken. "I learned so much." George Abbott has done over 100 shows on Broadway. In 1983, at the age of 96, he won several awards for his hit revival of ON YOUR TOES and now, at 101 years old, is still directing.

Ken's meeting Maxine was prompted by two mutual Baltimorean friends, actresses Sharon Page and Karen Wittokur. They thought Ken and Maxine might hit it off because they shared the same interests. Although Ken and Maxine were from the same hometown, Ken had no recollection of ever having seen her. "I got up enough nerve to call," remembers Ken. "I was immediately fascinated with her voice: bright, energetic and older sounding. I pictured someone very tall, thin and angular. When we met I was surprised to see the exact opposite: five-feet tall, Maxine was petite with a Lillian Russell hour glass figure, looking much younger and 'girlish' than her 23 years."

They had been seeing each other almost two years when Ken said, "Maybe, now, we should just 'dive' in and produce." Ken was about to be unemployed.

They had saved money, enough to get along for awhile. They had a lot of unemployment coming to them. They were living modestly.

On a part-time basis Maxine had been furthering her knowledge of scripts by working as a reader for the literary agent Leah Salisbury.

"We had come to know several people who kept saying that when we were going to produce, they wanted to invest. (You never know if that's for real or not.) We decided it was for real enough to give us courage to set out as producers. If they turned out not to be serious investors, at least we were steamed up enough to find others to invest. Fortunately, most of them meant what they said. Some have been with us ever since.

"Having decided we were going to start producing, we called several literary agents around town. We said, "We're going to be producing now. We'd like to be invited to showcases. Can you send us scripts? We'd like to hear ideas. We want to find something we'd like to produce."

"Nothing happened. We got very frustrated.

CHAPTER SEVEN

We laid it out ourselves; we did the whole ad. At that time, 1969, a full-page ad in VARIETY was only $700. It had an incredible impact; the response was enormous. We got a call from novelist-playwright Jerome Weidman. He'd seen our ad in VARIETY that morning. He asked, 'Is this for real?' We said, 'Yes, it's we who put in the ad.' He said, 'Producers don't advertise like that. It's not done. Nobody ever does that." Ken said, "Well, we did.'

"We got a script from a guy in Ohio; it was a musical about World War II — gunner pilots in the South Pacific. Great idea for a musical. And he said that he had invented a theatre seat for the audience that would lean back and shake as if the audience members were in the airplane; it would swivel around and everything. He added that if we wanted to produce the show, he would sell us the seats at a 20% discount!

"Then, we got a guy in Oklahoma who had written a musical about life at the country club. The plot - the conflict - of the musical was that at a nine-hole country club, a faction wanted to make an eighteen-hole golf course. Some members didn't agree, and the city wanted to use the land for something else. The action was which faction would win!

The writer had gone so far as to write all the reviews. He wrote that Clive Barnes, then of The New York Times, would say, 'The best musical I've seen in years. It will run for season after season.' He had Walter Kerr's review; Doug Watt's review; he'd written them all. He added, 'If you want to read the book and hear the music, send $25. I'll be very happy to send them to you.' "Fortunately, we did get legitimate calls from agents and a lot of scripts. We even got a telephone call from a literary agent, Ellen Neuwald, who urged us to see a play about a quadriplegic. We saw it at the American Place Theatre in New York, and we were impressed by the quality even though we didn't see it as commercial. When we called the agent, we asked who represented the director. She replied, 'He's a client of mine, a young fellow from Yale. He's back in California now, working in Los Angeles as associate director of the Mark Taper Forum. His name is Tom Moore.'

"As it happened, we were planning a visit to Los Angeles. The agent arranged two things for us: meeting Tom Moore and seeing Sal Mineo's production of FORTUNE AND MEN'S EYES.

"We met Tom Moore, and I felt he was terrifically talented. I told Maxine, 'You know, we're going to work with him some day. I don't

45

know when, but some day we're going to work with him. He's our kind of talent, and he sees things the way we do.'

"We went to see the production of FORTUNE, and we got carried away with it. We thought it was a terrific production: Sal's direction of it and especially his casting. I need to get enthusiastic to produce something, a handle for selling it to myself as well as everyone else.

"We wrote Sal Mineo a note and included our ad from VARIETY. We told him we'd seen the production, and we asked if we could meet him after the show, backstage. We said that we really thought we could make this work in New York.

"My image of Sal Mineo from the press and from everything else I'd heard was of a hostile guy, not too bright. I was thinking that he might be like that, and we wouldn't want to work with anybody like that.

"We went backstage, and we didn't see him, at first. We identified ourselves and asked somebody if Sal were around. Sal came walking over, and we knew from the first word out of his mouth that our previous image him was all wrong."

Sal looked at Ken and Maxine and said, "You're my age! In fact, you're not even as old as I am. When I looked at that VARIETY ad with all the shows that you worked on, I thought you were going to be as old as the heads of the Theatre Guild. Let's go talk."

"We told him we'd like to do the play, if certain alterations could be made. Sal said, 'You know, I'd thought that it just didn't seem right, but I didn't quite know where to break it, two acts, or three acts?'

"Back in New York we began to go to work on that production. Sal directed. We raised the money for FORTUNE AND MEN'S EYES in a week, $50,000," said Maxine.

Greatly impressed, I asked them if they were the usual investors in Broadway shows?

Maxine said promptly, "No. We tended not to attract the Broadway investors. We developed a group of our own. There were people who knew what we were doing. They'd known us for a long time. Through our friends and their friends, there were those we could go to for money. They knew that we had experience working in the theatre, that we had a healthy respect for investors and how to put on a show for a budget.

CHAPTER SEVEN

Sal Mineo

We respected Paul Zindel, and loved his writing. Ken and I had said that we would love to produce a play of Paul's. A few months later we received a call asking if we'd be interested in co-producing a play by Paul Zindel (this question really meant, did we want to help raise money). So our first Broadway show was AND MISS REARDON DRINKS A LITTLE.

"They needed money; so we raised money for it and got co-producer status. Ken took the greater burden. He was more the salesman than I. I dislike that aspect of producing intensely. It's a challenge, but it's not one I relish."

Maxine continued, "We were involved in two crucial decisions that were very important to that show. It was the beginning of our careers, and it was still rough for us. As we were not general partners, meaning the legal ruling partners. We didn't have a whole lot of power in terms of decisions and casting. Although Julie Harris had been signed to star, there was controversy over who got second billing. Eileen Heckart had agreed to play the third sister; Estelle Parsons was to play the second sister. Although Eileen Heckart was playing the third sister, she demanded second billing.

"Estelle Parsons insisted on second billing. The general producers talked to Ken and me about it. Estelle Parsons had just created a sensation in the film BONNIE AND CLYDE, and she had won an Oscar as best supporting actress.

"Ken said, 'You've got to give second billing to Estelle Parsons; she'll sell tickets. Eileen is a respected actress, but her name won't sell tickets for you; Estelle Parsons will.' "

Maxine was instrumental in a second important contribution to the show. After the out-of-town opening in New Haven, Ken and Maxine were driving back into town with the producers who were complaining about the actress Rae Allen, playing the girlfriend. They were thinking of firing her and getting somebody else.

Maxine said, "Look, Rae is a good actress; it's going to take her time to build that character. Do you guys know what you want from that character?"

One of the producers admitted that the director was confused about that particular character in the way he wanted that character to behave.

Then Maxine said, "I don't know how you can expect Rae Allen to give the needed performance when the director doesn't know what

CHAPTER SEVEN

he wants the character to be. She's a very inventive actress and I think she should be allowed to let the performance grow. Don't replace her at least until the end of the Washington, D.C. tryout."

Rae Allen won a Tony Award for the role.

"Opening night we all were stunned by the unfriendly reviews. Julie Harris said that she would take the show on tour if we gave her a month's vacation. After three months, we closed the show in New York. Julie Harris took the summer off and then toured for a year. It's to Julie Harris' credit that the show did, indeed, make a healthy profit."

Ken Waissman and Maxine Fox with Dr. Phillip Markin (center)

CHAPTER EIGHT

"It was located in a basement," said Maxine. "The basement of a building that had been a trolley barn of some kind in a section of Chicago called Old Town, sort of like our Greenwich Village."

"You speak of GREASE, how it began?"

"I got a call," spoke up Ken, "from an old friend of mine, Phillip Markin, a former college roommate who was studying orthodontics in Chicago. We had produced FORTUNE AND MEN'S EYES, and we'd co-produced AND MISS REARDON DRINKS A LITTLE, which was about to tour that fall, but it was August of 1971, and a low point for us. We were getting discouraged. He and his wife happened to go to see a showcase production of GREASE. Yes, it had the same title, GREASE, but it was more of a play than a musical; it was 70% book and 30% music. There were no central characters, but it was about the 1950's and going to high school. Jim Jacobs and Warren Casey had written it. They were 1950's buffs at a time when no one seemed interested in that decade. They had heard some fifties songs at a party one night, and they started to improvise a satirical song. This song eventually became Beauty School Dropout.

"Their friends laughingly told Jim and Warren, 'You know so much about that period. Have you two ever thought about writing a play about it?'

"Both Jim and Warren were professional actors, but were not working often, even though they had Actors Equity cards.

"Jim had been in a touring company of NO PLACE TO BE SOMEBODY; he had been working as a copywriter for an ad agency; Warren had been in a couple of shows, but now was a buyer of lingerie in a department store."

For the neighborhood amateurs it was a hobby; they weren't seriously interested in acting. The group was made up of housewives;

professional people, people with day jobs of one sort or another. The shows they put on might run for a few weekends. It was nonprofit.

"Our dentist friend, Phil, in telephoning me, said, 'This workshop is in a little theatre here in Chicago which seats 100 people on the floor on newspaper. There are no seats. There is no real stage. The performance takes place on the same level as the audience, right on the floor.'

"Phil added, 'There are some funny things. I don't know if it's for New York, because it's really rough. An amateur show. But it might be something to look at.'"

Ken mentioned it to Maxine, and they checked around town to see if anybody had heard about this workshop that was being done in Chicago. A couple of people said, "Yes, they'd heard about it. They thought the authors had some talent, but that it was an amateur production, not that good."

"Phil called us back, 'When are you going to come to Chicago?'"

Ken said, "Oh, I don't know. Everybody says it's just a piece of garbage."

Phil agreed, "Sure it is, but the idea's really terrific. It's worth seeing. Anyway, you can spend a day with us. We'll have a fun time. Remember when we were going to high school, the fellows with the ducktail haircuts and the girls with cinch belts and spongy bobby sox? Although in Baltimore, we called them 'drapes' and 'drapettes,' the rest of the country called them 'greasers.'"

Maxine and Ken both thought that it might be something to look at.

They flew out to Chicago. There was a heatwave, 90 degrees; humid as anything. They arrived, went down long, narrow steps, and were given a piece of newspaper with which to sit on the floor. There was no air conditioning in this basement.

The show started. Everything they had heard was true. There was a three piece band, but no music had been written down for the orchestra. The musicians were 'jamming.'

Ken said, "I couldn't hear the lyrics half the time; it was difficult to make out the melody. The plot just went on and on and on. (We later learned that the script that they were from was voluminous, including all the discards.) We could have gone out, had a hamburger, come back much later, and we really would not have missed anything. There was no central character. It was just a bunch of high

CHAPTER EIGHT

school kids being depicted on stage. Some scenes did end up in the Broadway show of GREASE: the pajama party, the high school dance, although each had been considerably changed.

"There were poor songs, and there were fabulous songs, for example: Grease Lightnin', Beauty School Dropout, We Go Together. Magic Changes was just background music as if heard on a radio. Because it was background music on a tape, the band was not drowning it out; I was able to hear and love it."

They were sitting there watching when suddenly they began not to notice that these were amateurs. They were not actors, but, they sure looked right for the roles they were playing. They gave Ken and Maxine an image which stayed with them when they were casting the Broadway show.

"The scenery was of brown paper on which the cast, themselves, had painted a few windows. Drip marks still showed. One such brown paper set represented the cafeteria. Another set of brown paper just said, 'Street.' Very simple. But after a few minutes, we weren't seeing the brown paper with the drip marks. We were seeing our own high school cafeteria, our own high school steps, the gym. We didn't see a young housewife trying her darndest to be an actress and to sing a song. We felt no embarrassment because of their enthusiasm; they were having a great time. We began to see girls that we'd known in high school. The fellow who used to sit two seats in front me, and a girl who used to hang out at the drug store. The characters that the authors had attempted to create had reality for us. We had begun to identify with them."

After the performance they met with the authors, Jim Jacobs and Warren Casey, and they told them that they loved the idea, but that they wanted to do it as a Broadway musical.

"As a play, it didn't hold up," said Maxine. "It was neither drama nor comedy. But as a musical, we thought it could be something special, if it were done really well.

"Both of you have talent, and although you haven't written before, we'll gamble you'll be able to rewrite. You know, the biggest challenge is 'Can you rewrite?' Rewriting is going to be required right up to the opening."

Ken said, "It was instinct that prompted us to want to do the show." Maxine added, "It was a feeling about Jim and Warren."

"If you agree," said Ken, "to work with us on this, we'll give you guidance. You'll have to write a full musical score. Some songs are great and can stay; some characters have to be cut; we have to find central characters. The piece has to be given a certain structure. So, if you're willing to move to New York and to work, we'll produce it."

It was a tough decision for Warren and Jim. It meant giving up their jobs.

"We don't have to make any new statement or go in any other direction, except the direction that you seem to be intending it to go," said Ken to Warren and Jim. "To me, it's like a dress on a dummy in a dress shop, cut but not sewn; all the pins and all the chalk marks are there. The hems are not in, but one can see that it can be a terrific dress just by finishing it." And said Ken, "That's exactly what we see in your piece. It needs to be finished."

Encouraging Jim and Warren further, Ken added, "The semi-documentary approach gives uniqueness to the Chicago production. The kids looked real when they made their entrances."

"They looked as if they came right off the street," Maxine added. "That was part of the charm, because it looked as if someone had opened a cedar chest, and the characters had crawled out for a few hours. But that they were going right back into storage at the end. That was the style we want for a full Broadway musical."

Jim and Warren liked that. They made an instant decision; they agreed to move to New York to start working on GREASE from scratch.

"When we announced in The New York Times that a Jim Jacobs and a Warren Casey, completely unknown, had written a play with music and that we were going to make it into a musical called GREASE, people thought we were crazy."

Some people told them that the '50's would never appeal. They wouldn't be able to bring back the '50's, because nobody would ever want to look at those clothes again! Maxine interjected, "The thought of audiences getting excited by the show kept us going."

"Once Jim and Warren started rewriting, we realized that the characters Danny and Sandy need to be highlighted, and made leads with a 'tried and true' format: boy meets girl; boy loses girl; boy gets girl. We felt this gave the show a needed plot.

"We figured out how Sandy and Danny would get together, how they would break up, and how they would get back together again.

CHAPTER EIGHT

Hand-Jive sequence at the High School Hop

Barry Bostwick and the 1950's 'car' built around a golf cart.

Some characters were cut; some became secondary. New songs were written: Summer Nights came out of the meetings. Jim and Warren had written a Monster Mash which was slow, dreary, and funereal."

As they talked about the High School dance scene, Maxine and Ken remembered a dance they used to do in high school, the Hand Jive.

"Can you write a song about that?"

Jim came back the next day with a Hand Jive song which he had written that night.

In Chicago, the production had used a real car. In New York, productions are not allowed to bring an automobile into a theatre and on to the stage if the motor is turned on. Ken and Maxine didn't want a winch to move it, but they were still in love with the memory of the way it had looked in Chicago.

"True, we recalled that their production had trouble getting it out onstage, and it seemed to take forever to get it off. The whole show had come to a dead stop.

"But what were the alternatives? An an electric car? There were a lot of objections to that; it wouldn't work; stage hands were not going to get it on stage; it would cost too much for a single number."

Having made it central to the concept of the show, Ken countered with, "Then we'll have to use it in the second act as well. It's like reprising a good song; the audience will love it!"

A golf cart was used around which was built a '50's hot rod.

Jim and Warren responded by coming up with a scene at a drive-in-movie. So, out of that, the song Alone At A Drive-In Movie was born.

"It was to be Danny's car. He's the main character. So out of the discussion came the incident that Danny borrows his buddy's car. Danny says to Sandy, 'Gee, Sandy, I practically had to bust Kenickie's arm to get his car for tonight.' The dialogue told the audience how suddenly Danny happens to have a car; it said a lot about teenagers' closeness, their lending each other cars, clothes, and emotional support.

"Who would have anticipated the contribution that that one song, Alone At A Drive-In Movie would have on shaping the stage play GREASE!"

Word got around that Ken and Maxine were making progress with their production. "International Creative Management Talent

CHAPTER EIGHT

Agency (ICM), the author's agents, was hoping that we would take a package of their ICM clients. One of the first directors they tried to sell us was Michael Bennet. A CHORUS LINE was still quite a way off in the future, but already he was a full-fledged Broadway choreographer.

"However, with all due respect, we felt he was not right for GREASE. So Maxine (who had worked with him on A JOYFUL NOISE) called him on the phone and said, 'Michael, ICM keeps talking about you to direct and choreograph GREASE. Before we pursue this, I think there is something we need to talk about: conceptually; Ken and I don't feel GREASE should have a chorus, or performers whose primary talent is dance. We feel the show needs good actors who have great singing voices and who, hopefully, move well. Would you want to choreograph a show like that?"

Michael answered, "No, that's not my cup of tea for now."

ICM, however, kept digging in their files. It got to the point, finally, where Ken and Maxine had to say to ICM, "Look, if ICM wants to produce the show, they should put up the money!"

Even before they had a director for GREASE, they had approached choreographer Patricia Birch. Maxine had thought of Patricia Birch with whom she had worked in YOU'RE A GOOD MAN, CHARLIE BROWN.

Ken said, "Maxine had taken me to see an off-Broadway production THE ME NOBODY KNOWS, for she wanted me to see Pat Birch's work. I fell in love with her work and with her. She showed an incredible talent for making non-dancers dance. She confessed that that's what she does. For years she hated to admit she makes actors dance. She works off the acting beats. She doesn't come in with her dances already fully prepared. She works them up with the actors."

The authors were getting pressure from different sources. As Ken tells it, "They were advised to watch out for us, that we weren't experienced producers. A lot of pressure came from ICM, saying, 'Be careful of Ken and Maxine's choices.' " Maxine and Ken overcame these potential estrangements.

However, Ken and Maxine decided that Pat Birch as choreographer would be just right, because she wouldn't give GREASE too slick a patina. Pat would be able to create rough edges; Maxine and Ken wanted that quality for GREASE.

Bernie Jacobs, Pat Birch, Maxine Fox, Jerry Schoenfeld

CHAPTER EIGHT

"Pat was reluctant to commit herself to the show at first. Pat said, 'I don't know that much about the period, the fifties.' She had never been approached on a show before where there was no director as yet. She said, 'Suppose you choose a director who doesn't want to work with me or vice versa?'

"It was very difficult to convince Pat Birch that we would not take a director unless he and she could work together."

Later Pat Birch had said, "You know, we were with Jim and Warren, and Ken and Maxine in my living room. The beer cans were floating around; Jim was playing the guitar, and not too well. It was my husband, Bill, who first thought GREASE had something. I had found it difficult to visualize the show from the rough audio tape."

On another occasion Ken smilingly said, "Imagine a show composed on a guitar! Over the years, so many people writing articles on GREASE have said, 'Oh, I want to have a photo of Jim and Warren sitting at the piano, working on the show.' I always had to say, 'Neither can play the piano.' "

They began seeking a director. For sometime none of the directors they talked to seemed to understand the show. Gerald Freedman was one of the directors they decided they'd like to talk to about GREASE. They invited him up to hear the music and go through the score. Maxine and Ken told him what they had in mind for the show. By then, they had a draft of the book of GREASE to give him. Ken said that he thought Jerry would be more into it than some other directors simply because he had been the original director of HAIR.

As they gave Jerry a script, Jerry said, "Terrific, I'll read it, and I will let you know."

They chatted some more and shook hands. "When Jerry left the room," said Ken, "he left the script on the table! He had completely forgotten to take it."

About two days later, Ken received a call from Jerry. Jerry said, "I read it, and decided that it's not for me."

Ken adds, "I don't even know if he recalls it, but we really roared over that one."

They talked to more directors and were getting nowhere. One night, about 2 a.m., Maxine and Ken were talking, and Ken said, "Listen, you know, maybe this is the right project for Tom Moore." The next morning they called Tom's agent, "Where can we get in touch with Tom Moore? Where is he now?"

Director Tom Moore with Ken Waisman

CHAPTER EIGHT

The agent said, "He's back in California."

Ken and Maxine called Tom and told him about the show, that they wanted him to come east. He said he would. Tom flew in from the coast, and Ken and Maxine introduced him to Jim and Warren. He read the script and heard the music. Although Tom had grown up in the period, he hadn't identified with the 'greaser' types, and he found the characters very unattractive. Ken countered with, "You don't have to like the period. Jim and Warren know everything about the period. What we want you for is to put the show on stage. The characters may be unappealing to you the way Jim and Warren have written them. What we want from you through casting and work on the script is to make them likeable."

Ken and Maxine felt that by the time all would be finished, the kids were going to be appealing. Otherwise, GREASE wouldn't work; the audience had to love them.

Ken and Maxine convinced Tom Moore that he was the director for the show. In signing him they took another major step in transforming the Chicago workshop production into a major Broadway musical.

But first, Tom was to meet choreographer Birch. Patricia Birch was getting edgy. She didn't know if she wanted to do GREASE. Tom was late, which gave Patricia ammunition for withdrawing. She said to Ken and Maxine, "Here's this kid who can't even get here on time."

"Pat was impatient to get to her appointment with John Houseman." added Ken.

When Tom arrived, Maxine and Ken sat them on the couch together. "We practically had to force them to start talking, but once they started, Pat forgot about her appointment with John Houseman."

Tom Moore and Pat Birch hit it off well and Ken and Maxine felt they had a perfect team.

"Then Warren decided that he did not like Tom Moore, as director, and he didn't know how they could really work with him. What aggravated the situation was that Tom tended to talk more to Jim than to Warren. Jacobs was very outgoing and Casey quite shy. So another meeting was set in which Tom focused directly on Warren. Let's face it; this is what show business is about."

The show was coming together very fast. By Thanksgiving, they had a director and a choreographer. They hired a staff, and began casting in early December.

Ken, Maxine, Tom and Pat auditioned 2,000 actors for the 16-member cast for GREASE. "We were tearing our hair out. We did hear a lot of talented people. Most didn't physically fit the roles we were casting. Early on we'd learned that onstage, real teenagers looked like babies; we had to cast actors in their twenties. We listened to actors who were terrific at acting, but couldn't sing. We weren't looking for dancers, but so many actors who both sang and acted well couldn't move at all. It was very frustrating."

GREASE went into rehearsal in February. They had decided not to take the show for an out-of-town tryout. They had the tryout right at the Eden Theatre.

The Eden Theatre, for years, had been the home of the Phoenix Theatre on Second Avenue, New York. For first previews of the musical GREASE, Ken and Maxine tried to get theatre people not to come; people they knew and backers were not allowed; they strived to keep agents away. They were fully aware that after the first dress rehearsal, panic had set in, for when the curtain came down, Pat Birch had said, "Christ, I don't want to do this goddamned show!"

Maxine said, "Only your worst enemy comes to your first performance! Among those 'enemies' are the out-of-work costume designers, scene designers; they always show up at the first preview. No one seems to know why."

Ken remembers, "The preview of GREASE did not go well, but we saw the problem. We pulled a fast one on the crepe hangers; we made major changes in the show before the critics got to it. We had two weeks in which to rewrite and restage. GREASE was put together in three and a half weeks of rehearsals, and two and a half weeks of previews. An unusually short time. The only reason it was done and done well within that short a time was due to the fact we didn't know it couldn't be done in that short a time!"

After the first preview, all involved with the show were really in a blue funk. An usher happened to be coming up the aisle: she saw their faces and said, "I don't know what you guys are worried about. This is going to be a hit!"

In chorus, all said, "How do you know?"

The usher said, "Because I'm looking around the theatre, and I see no programs left."

"This is an old theatre superstition; unfortunately not always true," said Ken.

CHAPTER EIGHT

Still, the authors were jittery. The director was a nervous wreck.

Ken later reminisced to me, "When I first was working in show biz, I decided I wanted to hear audience comment. The first show I worked on was a show that George Abbott had directed: it was trying out in Philadelphia. It was intermission, and I started walking around in the theatre lobby. I wanted to get the sense of what people were feeling about the show, the performance. I heard this one woman talking. She said, 'It's fabulous! It's absolutely wonderful. I just think it's terrific! And you can wear it with anything.' So much for intermission scoop.

"Previews are a time when creative people are the most unhinged."

Maxine and Ken were standing there thinking, "Oh, my God! What's going to happen now?"

One of the things that bothered Ken about the show was that it didn't have the size that he thought it was going to have. Ken wanted the show to feel like a full Broadway musical. Somehow, it seemed like a small off-Broadway romp. At this time, the band was up on the platform onstage. Ken thought if thy put the musicians in the orchestra pit the production would feel bigger. Director Tom Moore asked Ken to promise that if he felt it didn't work Ken would move them back onstage despite the cost. Ken was so sure it would solve this first major problem that he promised Tom. However, from then on for 3,388 performances on Broadway, and for all their other GREASE productions, the band was always in the orchestra pit.

At the next day's rehearsal, the authors were at the back of the house with their agent. The director wasn't talking to the authors; the authors weren't talking to the director.

Ken walked over to Jim and Warren and said, "I've been thinking that the beginning of the first act is top-heavy. What if we take the Yuck number out? It really doesn't work."

At this point, Pat Birch happened to be walking by. She was going to be one of Ken's allies (so he thought); she had agreed that it was not a good song.

Pat said, "Well, wait a minute. What about the terrific stage business I've done with the kids, their books and lockers."

Tom came over to Jim and Warren. Ken and Maxine walked away. For twenty minutes, the three talked. The next day, Jim and

Warren came in with a whole new scene, eliminating the Yuck number. Pat Birch's stage business was incorporated, however.

Now everybody was talking to everybody else.

"Previews are a time when the creative people are walking on eggs," said Maxine. "The director, the choreographer, the designers feel they are up on the stage with the performers and are totally exposed.

"The song that sounded so terrific at a backer's audition and made one say, 'What a wonderful song!,' all of a sudden, in front of an audience, just doesn't work."

So GREASE went through changes. "But you have to be careful," said Maxine.

"In an effort to eliminate 'dull' moments, Tom and the authors wanted to cut a scene between three actors that had not worked. But I reminded them that the scene was put into the show in the first place to give the audience information it needed about each of those characters and their relationship. So the purpose had to stay, even though the scene was changed."

Other scenes were changed; songs removed. There were musical numbers that Pat hadn't finished staging. "She not only works off the actors, she works off the audience. But she did finish staging all of her numbers before the last week of previews!" said Ken.

GREASE came together: all those little drops of water became a puddle. The audience suddenly saw the a working show, and that happened in the middle of the second week of previews.

"Now comes the horrible night, opening night," said Ken and Maxine.

During the opening night of GREASE, a lady in the audience fainted during the second act. Tom Moore came over to Ken and said, "I've become an animal!"

Ken said, "What are you talking about?"

Tom hissed, "I wanted to stomp on her. How dare this lady faint and interrupt our opening!"

In those days one always knew when it was opening night. Before the curtain calls had started, even before the curtain was down, a third of the house got up and left. That's the press. The cast was bowing to backs of the critics, who are going to decide their fate and the fate of the show.

CHAPTER EIGHT

The original cast of GREASE.

Barry Bostwick as Danny Zuko, Ilene Kristen as Patty Sincox, the cheerleader in the original production of GREASE.

"We turned on the television set at 10:15 p.m. and a critic, came on the air — he thought GREASE was awful! Another face came on the screen to say, 'The worst thing I've ever seen opened tonight at the Eden Theatre!'" Ken adds, "That was this reviewer's best line."

Someone called from The New York Times typesetting room to read off the Clive Barnes review. Ken and Maxine got on the phone to hear it: "Last night at the Eden Theatre, GREASE opened. A musical about the fifties. The only thing I remember about the fifties was that 1959 was a very good year for burgundy. I sat through the entire show, and I didn't know what I was watching." At the end he reversed himself by saying, "It may have a run."

Tom remained very calm. Tom, as a director, is great in a crisis. He said quietly, "You know, we may be just all right. We don't have all the reviews yet. Let's keep calm."

The Daily News review arrived, and it was a rave. All were very happy about that. They decided to meet in the morning, talk about what they might be able to do with the reviews, and learn what the ticket sales were like at the box office.

Opening night was over. The director, the choreographer, the authors had delivered their show. The major thing now had to come from the producers.

"Sometimes, the right thing for the producer to do is to close the show. The producer may not be taking anything in at the window; he has to meet cast payrolls, stagehands' payrolls, musicians' payrolls, enormous bills in one week. He is, personally responsible, liable. He may have a liability of $100,00.00 against him before he has time to post the notice to close the show," said Ken, rather breathlessly.

Maxine said, "This is where the 'worm turns' and we, the producers, are most sensitive and raw. We have to make choices that will affect hundreds of people."

"Sometimes producers recognize that there's a reason for keeping the show running, and they should put great effort into promoting it. The reviews provide a tool: if there are enough good ones. Reviews generally lose their sting two months into the run. If you can survive that period of time without losing your shirt, imaginative publicity and advertising can get people into the theatre," is Ken's point of view. "That is, if they truly like the show." To this, Maxine readily agrees.

CHAPTER EIGHT

"You may have to 'paper' for a full house, so that people go out and tell other people. You may feel a 'build' in your show through 'word of mouth'."

The next morning after the opening, Ken and Maxine had to decide what to do. Their attorney was very concerned. He was worried as to how to protect Ken and Maxine.

Some years later, Ken and Maxine were to tell IASTA's Musical Theatre Studio members they had done an incredible thing, and they had successfully pulled it off.

A critic of the New York Post had hated GREASE; he had really loathed the show. Ken and Maxine got the idea to take the Daily News review, which was a rave, have it set in the New York Post type, and use the New York Post masthead as it usually is above the review. Instead of the New York Post critics picture, they substituted the Daily News critic's picture and his name.

They placed it as an ad in the New York Post.

"The guy who made up the page in the composing room thought that he was looking at his owns paper's review! He had it printed opposite another review in the paper that was set up the same way. He had forgotten to label it as a bonafide advertisement! It went through the paper as though it were one of their reviews.

"The next day," says Ken, "Maxine and I got calls about the great review in the New York Post. It worked!" Several years later, Waissman did the same thing again...reprinting Clive Barnes' review of AGNES OF GOD in the Daily News.

They did not have enough money, actually, in the bank to back up the paychecks they had to issue on Thursday night. If worse came to worst, they could cover the paychecks using the Actors Equity Bond that had been posted. They were sitting there wondering what to do. Maxine and Ken believed in their show. They believed that it could appeal to the public. However, they had to do something, for they were the only people in that room who were absolutely sure about what they were doing. The money they were taking in at the box office was a little more each day. "The gross from the week was higher than the previous week, and we had some good quotes from the reviews for advertisements." Maxine said.

The first thing they did was to lay out some of the ads. Secondly, when friends, backers, and people in the business called for house seats, they had instructed their assistant to say, "We have no house seats until the end of the month." Ken said, "That was a bit of a trick, because there were those in show business who were saying the show's closing. We decided to throw these 'doubting Thomases' a clinker. Anyone who thought that they could get down to see GREASE on 'easy-to-get' house seats, were not going to get them.

"Suddenly, there was a different image for the show. It's amazing how this supposed shortage of seats got to the press. It worked. Every situation is different. It doesn't mean it would necessarily work for another show."

The sale of tickets at the Eden Theatre kept growing. Still, they 'papered' (gave complimentary tickets), but to people who were not connected with the theatre industry. The theatre looked sold-out. They broke even the first week. Three weeks later, they knew the show was going to run. Each week, GREASE made a larger profit.

Realizing that when summer came on, it would be harder and harder to attract an audience to the off-Broadway Eden. Ken and Maxine began exploring moving the show to Broadway. The real future for GREASE lay in moving uptown.

"Maxine and I wanted to make people think, even though GREASE was down at the Eden Theatre, that it was still a 'Broadway' musical."

The Tony Awards (Broadway's equivalent to the Oscars) were coming up. The word was that GREASE was not going to be eligible, because it had been decided that a show down on Second Avenue and 12th Street would not qualify, even though the show was on full Equity Broadway production contracts. GREASE was also not eligible for the Obie Awards (which are presented to off-Broadway shows) because it was using Broadway contracts. Ken asked his staff, "Well, if they're not going to make us eligible, what can we do to create a lot of noise about it?"

Ken answered his own question, "We are always looking for good publicity; anything that will get the show in the newspapers. We'll sue them! Anybody in this country can sue anybody else, and this would be great copy."

They decided they would sue the League of New York Theatres; the Tony Committee; they would even sue ABC Television which carried the program for the Tony Awards. But not just sue; they proposed to get an injunction against releasing the nominations. "A silly case, in that we knew we couldn't win" confided Ken.

CHAPTER EIGHT

They were sitting there in the office with press representative Betty Lee Hunt. Before they would actually file a suit, they decided to send a letter to every member of the Tony Committee, telling them that the producers and actors of GREASE, all concerned, were highly insulted. They knew that they were, in substance, a Broadway show, because the show was on Broadway contracts.

Exclaimed Ken, "How dare they say just because geographically we weren't in the right area that we're not a Broadway show! If they did not make us eligible by noon the next day, we were going to file suit. To make sure that the letter was read, we had decided to hand-deliver a copy of it to every single theatre section newspaper man in the tri-state area: New Jersey, New York State, Connecticut."

Carbon copies of the letter were sent to every entertainment editor at every newspaper. The first response came from the League of New York Theatres, co-sponsors of the broadcast. "How dare you do this! What are you trying to work? If you thought you had a problem, why didn't you come to us?"

Calmly, Ken said to the person on the telephone, "We did."

"If we have to fight, let's not battle in the papers. Fight with us alone!"

Ken replied, "You dismissed us."

"Well, if you were eligible, you would have to pay Broadway advertising rates."

Ken replied, "Well, we are paying Broadway ad rates."

"You might have to pay for a few more musicians."

Ken fired back, "We can afford them. We can also afford to sue."

"I've never heard of such a thing. You'll never get nominated. We'll never allow that show to be eligible. You're wasting our time."

A call came back about ten minutes later. Alexander H. Cohen, producer for many years of the Broadway Tony Awards, called back and said, "We've got to talk about this. We're going to call an emergency meeting. This action you are planning to file at noon, can it wait until 4 o'clock?"

Ken put him on 'hold' while he, Maxine and their press agent, Betty Lee, talked about it.

Ken came back on the line and said, "Alex, we'll wait until 2 o'clock."

Ken figured that the worst thing that could happen now was to become eligible; GREASE would never be nominated for anything. "Better to get as much newspaper space as possible."

"We promised Alex that until 2 o'clock we'd not give out any more stories."

In fifteen minutes, Alex Cohen called, "I just want to tell you the whole thing has been a terrible mistake, an oversight. We had a meeting with the Tony Committee and with Richard Barr, the President of the League of New York Theatres (now the League of American Theatres and Producers).

The whole thing is an oversight. You're going to be eligible. I'll send confirmation over by messenger. The whole thing was a mistake. You are eligible, and when the Tony Committee receives all of the shows for consideration, GREASE will be right there. Will you promise me something?"

Ken asked, "What's that?"

"Since you are eligible, and since it was a mistake, and since we apologized, will you not give any more stories to the newspapers?"

Ken replied, "I will not give any stories to the newspapers. A deal is a deal. You're making us eligible. That's what we're asking for."

Ken meant to keep his word and he did.

"There was talk on the Rialto that GREASE wouldn't be nominated for anything," said Ken.

Ken and Maxine went on vacation, their first in a long time. During that week, Tony nominations were to be announced. They were not even thinking about them.

Maxine and Ken received a long distance call from New York City; it was from Betty Lee. Tony nominations had come out that morning: GREASE had been given seven of them!

"We were 'freaked out,'" said Ken.

As producers, Ken and Maxine wanted to move GREASE where the action was: West 44th Street or West 45th Street, which have the largest concentration of legitimate theatres. Most of these playhouses are owned by the Shubert Organization. A show that's located on one of these two streets automatically seems more important than a show at the Lyceum Theatre to the east of Times Square, or the Martin Beck Theatre, even though it's on 45th Street, West of Eighth Avenue. In those days, Ken points out, "Just about five steps in the wrong direction; and you were considered a 'death house.'"

CHAPTER EIGHT

From the original GREASE cast: Kathi Moss, Barry Bostwick, Dorothy Leon, Alan Paul, Jim Weston

"Every show is a 'child' unto itself," said Maxine. "What works for one show may not work for another show." She added, "The period after opening night could be titled 'Bringing Up Baby.' "

Maxine and Ken had told their staff that they had decided to move GREASE right to 44th Street, at the beginning of June. The Shubert Organization did not necessarily believe in GREASE. Some of the Shubert people had come down to Second Avenue to see it, and they had walked out. Lawrence Shubert Lawrence had liked GREASE. When the other representatives had left, he had stayed.

"Our show was doing good business," said Ken. "The Shuberts couldn't deny that and they were to have a few empty theatres during the summer."

Warren Caro, a former executive of the Shubert Organization said to Ken and Maxine, "A lot of tourists, with their kids, come to New York when schools are out. So, maybe we can give you a theatre for the summer. What theatre would you like to have?"

Ken and Maxine said, "The Broadhurst."

"Well, you can't move into the Broadhurst. That's going to be booked."

Ken and Maxine remained firm. "Well, we never wanted to move anyway. Our General Manager talked us into it. We're only up here because we thought we'd get the Broadhurst." They promptly left. "We were so arrogant in those days!," confesses Ken.

"Warren Caro came out after Ken and Maxine and asked them to wait a few minutes while he had a conference."

He returned shortly and said to Ken and Maxine, "Okay, you can have the Broadhurst through November."

Ken and Maxine said, "Fine. But, where are you going to put us in November?"

Ken and Maxine agreed to go into the Ambassador Theatre in November.

Ken adds, "There was a clause that said the Shuberts could ask our permission to book the Ambassador. But then, when November came, if we couldn't agree on a theatre, we would be free to go to another theatre owner.

"We were poised to move into the Broadhurst, and we went to the Shubert office at the appointed time, 5 o'clock for the signing. It had been discovered that Lawrence Shubert Lawrence had not signed. The place was in a panic. They had no idea where Lawrence

CHAPTER EIGHT

Shubert Lawrence was. They called all over town. There was no sign of him. We sat there waiting.

"Finally, they located him; we walked into the office; he sat down to sign the contract and flipped through it. He didn't seem to look at anything, but he suddenly saw the provision where we had a concession percentage clause."

At the Eden Theatre, Waissman and Fox's GREASE company had a percentage of the concessions; drinks, programs, etc. In the Shubert house, a percentage of concessions had never been given to a production.

Mr. Lawrence turned to Warren Caro and he said, "Warren, we never give a percentage of the concession!"

Warren says, "That's right."

Lawrence Shubert Lawrence said, "Well, we can't give it to them. This can't be in the contract. How come we're giving them a percentage of the concessions?"

Warren Caro replied, "Why don't you just sign it, Larry, and we'll talk about it afterwards."

"But, we've never given a percentage. Why are they going to get a percentage of the concession?"

Warren replied, "Well, Larry, they wanted all of the concessions, but we got them down to 25%!"

Larry mumbled, "Very good, Warren."

GREASE was moving to the Broadhurst. It was exactly the same size theatre with almost exactly the same layout as the theatre the show was leaving, the Eden. No critics were to be invited. "It was not an opening. It was just moving from one theatre to another," said Ken.

They started running ads: 'See it now at the Eden Theatre, so you can see it again at the Broadhurst.'

"At the end of the final week at the Eden, we did 60% capacity. At the end of our first week at the Broadhurst, we had achieved 80% capacity. Our move had been successful."

CHAPTER NINE

GREASE was now on Broadway. Ken and Maxine decided to produce another show, OVER HERE!.

How did you come upon the idea for that musical?

"It started with a record," answered Maxine. Ken added, "The Sherman Brothers sent us a record of their 40's musical. They did the the show in Los Angeles, in an off-off-Broadway type situation. It was called VICTORY CANTEEN. They went into a studio with twelve musicians, no vocals, and recorded the music. We put it on a record player, and all of a sudden all that warm brass sound came out of the record player. It felt so sensational to hear those sounds again. We decided to send for the rest of the material. They sent us the music with the book. We read the book of the show; it was too much like a sketch for Broadway. But, we thought that if we could work with them there was a show there.

"We called the Sherman Brothers to arrange a meeting with them out in California. We never option material for a show without meeting those who wrote it, because if you sense you can't work with them, no matter what they've written, it's not going to happen. There has to be a chemistry there, and you've got to be able to communicate.

"We sat down with them. We told them that we thought there was a show in there somewhere. We liked them a lot. We came back to New York. It was 1973 and we were preparing the London company of GREASE; that year we were traveling all over the place with GREASE.

"Busy as Pat and Tom were, we had them read the script. We practically locked them in a room to get them to read it. Then we talked, and they agreed that the show written for California was much too small, that it would not stand up to Broadway expectations.

Patti Andrews

Maxene Andrews

CHAPTER NINE

"We had another meeting with the Sherman Brothers, and we all said what we felt about it. To Bob Sherman's eternal credit, he got up and said, 'You're telling us that our five-year-old daughter can't dance well enough for Broadway.' We said, 'Yes, that's what we're saying.' So he said, 'Okay, let's get rid of VICTORY CANTEEN! and start over!'

"The original two writers dropped out," said Maxine. "We asked Will Holt to do the book, and we built from scratch a show based on the sound: a musical that was set in the '40s about the homefront."

Ken, you were growing up with an awareness of this type of music?

"Born into the middle of World War II, I knew the sounds of Glen Miller. This was original music, but in that vein. I could suddenly picture that whole big band rising up the way they used to. It inspired me. Had my parents not been playing those big band records and all that kind of stuff, I might not have reacted to or related to VICTORY CANTEEN the way I did."

Maxine said, "Ken and I decided we wanted to do the musical with both of the Andrews Sisters, the symbols of the World War II era (the third Andrews sister, Laverne, had died years earlier). We met with the two of them. In negotiations, Patti Andrews wanted a lot more money than Maxene Andrews."

Ken added, "That's right. We offered an equal salary and an equal percentage; they couldn't seem to figure out how to divide it up; 50-50 was evidently not satisfactory. So during that period, it was impossible to make a deal with them. We gave up the project."

Had nobody told you what it might be like working with the Andrews Sisters?

"We knew that there were certain difficulties, but we also had heard how badly they wanted to be on Broadway. We assumed that they were real pros.

"Sometime later, we happened to bump into Peter Witt, a very good agent. (He later went into producing.) He happened to ask how the Sherman Brothers' musical was coming. We said, 'We abandoned it. It was impossible to make a deal with the Andrews Sisters.' Peter thought it was such a wonderful idea, that it would be terrific for the Andrews Sisters' careers to be working again. He volunteered to see if he could be an intermediary. By then the Andrews Sisters seemed ready to make a deal. Everybody now wanted the show.

"It was agonizing making the deal with the two of them. After squeezing and pushing, Maxene agreed to accept a lesser amount of money. Then there was an article in Variety about how much Debbie Reynolds was making in IRENE. She was making 10% of the gross with a phenomenal guarantee. The Andrews Sisters had read that article. We had to go back in and negotiate the deal all over again for more money. But, we finally did get the contracts.

"They really had become excited. They had never before been on Broadway. It had been a dream of their's. They had played the Paramount Theatre, and when they had walked through Shubert Alley to the Piccadilly Coffee Shop and had passed the Shubert stagedoor, they had talked about one day wanting to play in that very theatre."

OVER HERE! was booked, after Philadelphia, into the Shubert Theatre. Maxene Andrews kept saying, "When I get to New York, it's going to be incredible. I'm going to be invited to all the parties. I'm going to get all kinds of gifts. They're going to take care of my dogs in Sardi's when I go there after the show." She was absolutely right. All of those things happened. They did get invited to all those parties. Maxene Andrews got more sweat shirts than she could wear. Patti Andrews got sheets and towels. It was an incredible thing. And they did take care of the dogs in Sardi's. But, as Ken says, 'hell is portable,' and they were not happy.

Ken said, "We put our show together in rehearsal, went out of town." Maxine Fox had said that they checked on the show GREASE repeatedly to see that it wasn't sagging or slipping. Producers should do that.

With all the responsibilities of keeping GREASE going, and at a quality level, was it a difficult decision to embark upon OVER HERE!, another big show?

Maxine answered, "It wasn't difficult at all. Oh, we got cries of abandonment from our GREASE cast, and we had a tour out at the time. There was a lack of focus for a period of time.

"When the two shows were running simultaneously, the greater attention was to OVER HERE!, simply because it needed us more as a new show coming to Broadway. It's like having two children. The baby of the family often gets more attention. You don't produce a show, wait until it closes, and then produce another show. It's an ideal to have more than one show running, but you have to be careful not to dissipate focus."

CHAPTER NINE

OVER HERE! played out of town?

Maxine continued, "Yes, in Philadelphia."

When did you and Ken become aware of the tension between the two Andrews Sisters?

"They got it together for out-of-town. We were slightly aware of it, but not really. After opening night, they became difficult. We got a fabulous set of reviews and we had them bound. We gave Patti and Maxene each a bound copy. When they flipped through them, they were not pleased; they threw the books across the room. Why? They hated the reviews, for the critics only wrote about them in one paragraph, and spent the rest of the time writing about the show and the other performances. They were furious.

"The show was a hit, it had gotten terrific reviews; everyone was running to see it. Guys from the Glen Miller band, Benny Goodman band, all the big bands of that period, were coming to see the show. Several said to us, 'Didn't you know that Patti and Maxene didn't get along, that there was a family squabble?'

"Patti's attitude was incredible. One Saturday, between matinee and evening performances, Carol Channing, who was in LORELEI at the time, came over to have dinner with Maxene and Patti in Patti's dressing room. We had heard about that; we stopped at the theatre that night; went into Patti's dressing room and said we hear Carol Channing came over during the matinee break today. Patti said, 'Yeah, it was terrific. I had Chinese food and Carol, of course, brought her own stuff.' How did it go, we asked. Patti said, 'Oh, it was great, except that she kept talking to me about how I should do press and everything.' I asked Patti what her reply was to Carol. Patti said, 'Well, I didn't say what I should have said, which was, if I were Carol Channing I'd have to do press also.'"

I had heard they had insisted on their own hair dresser; there was a conflict over wigs?

"The fellow that had been hired to do Patti's wig was not doing his job at all. He was not putting the wigs away; he was showing up late; he was leaving early. We decided that he had to be replaced. He had already been let go and Patti decided that she wasn't going to wear any wig on stage unless he was rehired. We weren't going to take him back; we had several choices of wonderful people to take care of the wigs. Patti had extremely short cropped hair and she actually went out on stage a couple of nights without her wig, and looked bald. The inefficient hair dresser was not rehired! So she went back to her wig thereafter.

"Their curtain calls used to bring the audience to their feet as they sang a medley of their old tunes with great big wonderful smiles. All the while, Patti was squeezing Maxene's arthritic fingers. Maxene Andrews, through the pain, was doing everything she could to smile and act as if the Andrews Sisters were still as American as apple pie."

"Not only would Patti squeeze her sister's fingers, but she pushed her down the stairs one day. It was just awful," added Maxine Fox.

"When the grosses began to falter, there was talk of going on the road. But the Andrews Sisters just weren't getting along. To tour, they wanted separate deals. Because of their carrying on, the insurance company cancelled the 'star insurance' policy we had taken on them. Bernard Jacobs of the Shubert Organization was willing to get an insurance policy for them from Lloyds of London, but we needed something in writing that, on tour, they would guarantee to live up to their contract and do reasonable publicity. In New York Patti had refused to do press. Maxene had been willing to do press. But you can't publicize an Andrews sister (which is the way Maxene is billing herself now, by the way)!

"Without these letters of intent, no deal with a theatre chain could be made. Nobody would gamble on their living up to their contract, and we couldn't ask anybody to take that risk. So, we closed the show and didn't tour."

"Ken and I are both fighters for the shows that we do. There was no way we were going to give up OVER HERE! if it's problems could have been solved. We bit the bullet," added Maxine.

She continued, "It had been like banging one's head against a brick wall. It was awful. We put up the notice to close; we knew we weren't going to take it down. In a way, we were relieved. This was a show which had all raves, and it was a production that wouldn't be profitable. It was absurd. OVER HERE! could have made money for everyone.

"Had we known, I'm sure we wouldn't have done OVER HERE!. But, we're glad that we did it. We're proud of it. On stage, for two hours every night, the Andrews Sisters gave the most wonderful performance. They were always fresh and always there. They were wonderful. The other twenty-two hours in the day, they acted like unhappy, sad, angry people. An incredible experience."

What happened to them since?

"We've heard little bits and pieces. Maxene has been doing a cabaret act; billing herself: Maxene Andrews, an Andrews Sister. Patti Andrews, as far as I know, is hanging out at a country club somewhere." (Several years later, Maxene Andrews made amends to Ken. They see each other on occasion.)

Ken, do you think they regret it today?

"Maxene Andrews does. As for Patti, she may still think it was her sister who caused the show to close, or that it was somebody else's fault; ours, or Actors Equity."

They must have made some money?

"They lost a lot of money by not touring OVER HERE!."

You spoke of a show that got great reviews, Ken. When you realized that it was going down the tubes, how did you feel?

"When you have stars like the Andrews Sisters, the press will only cover the show if they can have the Sisters. With Patti's unwillingness to do publicity, the 'noise,' so important to maintaining hit status, faded away. I felt anger and rage over a situation where stars were behaving in such an unreasonable, unprofessional, and self-destructive way. We had all worked very hard creating a show. We had received great success and were doing terrific business when we first opened. Much of the anger resulted from the helplessness I felt. It felt like their commitment to destroy the show and themselves was a stronger commitment than mine was to keep OVER HERE! going? The two siblings unresolved anger created chaos.

"After OVER HERE!, the legendary producer David Merrick said to me," continued Ken, "'You've just swung ten baseball bats. From now on all the stars you work with will feel very light.' He was absolutely correct. I've had wonderful and rewarding working relationships with stars ever since."

CHAPTER TEN

Disposing of film rights seems a complicated business; Ken, how did you handle the film rights to GREASE?

Ken replied, "GREASE opened February 14, 1972. Shortly after we had an offer from Paramount. The head of Paramount Productions wanted to get the movie rights, and an agreement to release the film by Christmas of '74.

"We said, 'Absolutely not. If the film came out while GREASE was still running, it would kill the show.' We convinced the authors to turn the deal down. Paramount's position was that a fifties thing was just a fad. If they didn't get it out fast (Paramount said), they might as well forget it. So they forgot about it - for then."

"A little while later, we were approached by Steve Krantz and Ralph Bakshi: they had a very interesting concept to do it as an animated film. Ralph Bakshi had done FRITZ, THE CAT and a couple of other features. He's a very talented man. They planned to release it in '75. Our writers very much wanted to go with that. Hollywood wasn't buying Broadway musicals at that moment. So, we rationalized that the two versions would be so different. The stage version would not be threatened.

"Ralph Bakshi was the one we admired. We had it put into the contract that if at any time Ralph and Steve split up, the rights would come back. They split up, and the rights came back to us. "Maxine and I were having lunch at Sardi's, and Allan Carr came in. He asked when the movie was coming out. We replied that it was not going to come out, because we had the rights back. He said he didn't know that.

"He was a big star manager in Hollywood, and had recently produced a movie. Carr said he just made a production deal with (of all studios) Paramount. He was interested in GREASE. We didn't know Allan Carr that well though we had been acquainted with him over the years. We did like his work. I liked his involvement in the Ann-Margret specials. I liked the fact that he was a really good promoter. We said, 'If you're really serious, Allan, call us at the office,' assuming that since he was also waving to '50,000 people' in Sardi's at the same time, that's the last we were going to hear of that.

"We got back to the office, and our receptionist said, 'There's a man on the line named Allan Carr. So Allan was serious. I set up a meeting with the agents for GREASE at ICM.

"The agents were not very keen, saying, 'Who's Allan Carr? He has a deal with Paramount. So what.' I said, 'We haven't had any other offers. Carr is recognized promoter.

"Negotiations began. The problem really was when the movie would come out.

"GREASE was making a lot of money on Broadway. There were also two touring companies. We were determined not to let anything interfere with its success. We wanted the release date of the film put way off. Negotiations took a long time. Allan assured us there'd be no problem with the release date. It was not important that the film get out fast.

"We talked with Allan about who should be in the film. We recommended John Travolta, who had, of course, been in the Broadway GREASE. Allan thought that it was an interesting suggestion, but as a TV name, not one that would be enough box office. We hoped that Allan would involve Robert Stigwood in the film soundtrack album. Meanwhile, we didn't know was that Stigwood was in the process of signing John Travolta to a three-picture deal. The first picture was set, SATURDAY NIGHT FEVER.

"We ended up having a battle with Carr and Paramount on the release date. We didn't want to kill the Broadway run. We wanted the opening around Christmas of '80. It was getting ugly, and the authors, Maxine, and I were fighting among ourselves. The release date is supposed to be a mutual decision between the author and the producer. The authors didn't want to lose the film. We finally went to arbitration, because we and the authors could not come to an agreement. Likewise, the authors, Maxine and I and Paramount and Allan Carr could not come to an agreement. So the opening of the film, set by arbitration, was set for June, 1978. The authors' agents were prepared to take a flat fee and then be done with it. We held out for a percentage of the gross. Our lawyer fought for it. Paramount thought GREASE, as a film, would be a long shot; so they ended up giving us 12 percent of the gross receipts after break-even in lieu of a large up-front fee. Our investors have been quite thankful.

"While the lawyers were in the midst of working out all of this, Maxine suggested that the lawyers demand a letter of credit to support the money that Allan Carr would owe all of us on this agreement. The authors' lawyers were reluctant to rock the boat, but somehow we got them to make the demand anyway. To take care of the money demand, Allan brought Robert Stigwood into the project. Without Robert Stigwood, there would have been no Bee Gees and no John Travolta.

"We were also able to get something else in the contract. We put it in as one of those things that you assume the 'other side' is going to catch. The clause read that there was to be no advertising until after the film opened in New York. That was absurd. After it opened in New York and had been reviewed, then they could advertise, but not before. No recordings were to be released until a specified time around the opening of the film. Paramount's lawyers did not pick up on this clause and the agreement was executed.

"We went to Europe in December, and when we got back messages from Paramount were waiting for us. Paramount's Vice-President of Worldwide Marketing, Gordon Weaver, wanted to have a meeting with us. It was very urgent!

"He came to see us because of that clause that had gone unnoticed. They had finally spotted it six months before the movie was to come out. He said, 'How can we not advertise until after the movie opens?'

"We responded, 'That clause was put in there to protect our show. We wanted the show protected until the very last minute. That's why it's there.'

"He said, 'It's going to be harmful to the movie, but I've got something that I would like to offer.'

"We said, 'What's that?' "

"If you allow us to start promoting the film in, let's say four, five, six weeks ahead of the opening, we would tie-in the Broadway show."

Ken said, "That sounds interesting. What else could you do for us?"

He replied, "I'm sure there must be something."

Olivia Newton-John with John Travolta and Ken Waissman

CHAPTER TEN

Maxine said, "What if there were a 30-second commercial for the Broadway show at each showing of the GREASE movie in the tri-state area including Philadelphia? And how about using the commercial whenever you show 'coming attractions' anywhere in the country."

He said, "I don't know."

Ken said, "We would put together that 30-second commercial ourselves if you would pay for it."

"Maybe we can do that."

Ken added, We're just doing a new TV commercial. We'd like to put it on the air this summer. Maybe Paramount could pay for the amount of the air time."

"To everyone's benefit, they gave us what we asked for."

On June 13, 1978, Paramount Studios went all out for this opening of the film GREASE at Grauman's Chinese Theatre. Maxine and Ken had arrived in a white Rolls Royce; for them the red carpet, the kleig lights, the celebrities from all over, the crowds of people had made this Hollywood opening an old-fashioned premiere.

"What was so exciting for us was that we had stuck to our guns. We had a vision that it would be refreshing and exciting and fun to spend a couple of hours being in a time capsule, living in the fantasies, the fears, the excitements of adolescence again for a couple of hours in the theatre. The thought of audiences' getting excited by the show we'd produced the way we'd hoped it would be kept us going. Our presence in Hollywood for the opening of the film GREASE was a pinnacle for us," said Maxine.

"Starring in the film was then the hottest star in the world, John Travolta. The enormous promotion made it very, very exciting. As we got out of the Rolls Royce, we saw thousands of people, fans, newspaper people. A reporter came up to us and said, 'I just want to ask you one question: How does it feel?'"

Ken replied, "Well, considering many people advised us not to do GREASE, that it would last only two weeks at best, I find that our standing here, under all these kleig lights, with every star in Hollywood out, and thousands of fans in the street, the most exciting night of our careers - so far!"

"After the premiere, all the limousines drove to the Paramount lot, down different roads to parties on three connecting sound stages. One sound stage was just like a high school gym; one was for dancing; and another had tables, chairs, and food stands. The party was so big,

John Travolta arriving for the Gala Performance.

On stage after the Gala performance: Barry Bostwick, Patrick Swayze, John Travolta

CHAPTER TEN

but it was never crowded. One never had to wait for food or drinks," said Maxine.

"The event actually started the spring before," says Ken. "Marilu Henner, who was starring in the hit television series TAXI, called: she suggested that if there was some way to get a plane to fly the original New York and National Tour cast members (those now in LA) to New York, they would want to perform the show that night. I thought, what a great idea!"

Ken and Maxine contacted Bruce Lucker and Klaus Incamp, professional event organizers based in Atlanta. They had organized the I LOVE NEW YORK promotion here and abroad. Ken and Maxine had gotten friendly with Bruce and Klaus when they and members of the New York GREASE cast had traveled to Amsterdam to participate in a big I LOVE NEW YORK event. Ken and Maxine engaged Lucker and Incamp to organize the GREASE Alumni Weekend. They began trying to promote an airplane to fly all former cast members to New York.

The key to all this was, of course, securing a free plane ride. Fortunately, PAN AM was just initiating an LA to NY route and agreed to co-host the weekend. They provided a 747 reserving the first class and business class sections exclusively for GREASE and, in addition, painted the logo on the side of the plane.

"We rehearsed the double casts in Los Angeles, because so many of the cast members were working there," Ken said.

On Friday evening, December 6th, 100 GREASE alumni, including John Travolta and Olivia Newton-John, gathered at the LA Airport for a special pre-flight reception. By bus, the alumni were taken out on the runway to board the plane. In order to decide who got what seat, all the names had been put in a hat and chosen at random. PAN AM had continuous catering of special menus. At one point in the flight, a group including Travolta and Olivia were sitting on the floor in the

Judy Kaye as Rizzo.

Marilu Henner as Marty singing Freddy My Love

aisle playing cards and Marilu Henner, having swapped clothes with one of the stewardesses, was serving hors d'oeuvres. Judy Kaye, today the Tony Award-winning star of PHANTOM OF THE OPERA, somehow managed to sleep most of the trip, reminding her fellow cast members "You have a show to do tomorrow!"

When the flight landed in New York at 6 a.m. Saturday morning, twenty-five limousines were waiting to whisk the alumni to the Sheraton Center Hotel where everyone was staying. After catching some sleep, those appearing in the performance that night were picked up and taken to the Royale Theatre for a press conference and a dress rehearsal.

Sunday morning at noon, an alumni brunch took place at the Sheraton Center. Former cast members, including Rex Smith, Ray De Mattsis, and Patrick Swayze, had put together a skit doing takeoffs on the score, with songs like Hebrew School Dropout for Beauty School Dropout, and so on. That evening everyone checked out and returned to Los Angeles as guests of PAN AM on the GREASE plane.

"We had been preparing this weekend for so long," remembers Ken. "It all seemed to go by so fast. In addition to my family and Maxine's family, I had friends there from every period of my life: from the neighborhood in Baltimore where I grew up; from high school; college; summer camp; the Peace Corps; and my early days in New York."

On December 8, 1979, another "gala" took place. This time it was in New York. On that evening GREASE surpassed FIDDLER ON THE ROOF and became the longest running show (play or musical) in Broadway history. The Royale Theatre was filled to capacity with celebrities, theatre colleagues, investors, friends, and 200 GREASE alumni, 100 of whom (including John Travolta and Olivia Newton-John) had been flown in from Los Angeles on a special PAN AM flight with the logo GREASE painted on the side of the plane.

The first National Company performed the first act. The cast included: Marilu Henner, Jeff Conaway, Candice Early, Judy Kaye, Michael Lembeck and Jerry Zaks.

The second act was performed by the original cast and included: Barry Bostwick, Carole Demas, Ilene Kristen, Alan Paul (of The Manhattan Transfer), Kathi Moss and Walter Bobbie.

At the curtain call Ken and Maxine came out onstage and introduced the current cast who, in costume, joined the others. As the

In Los Angeles, taking off for the GREASE alumni weekend. Front row: Ken Waissman, Pat Birch, Maxine Fox, Marilu Henner, John Travolta, Ellen Travolta (John's sister). Back row: Jeff Conway, Tom Moore, Ted Wass.

CHAPTER TEN

orchestra played Pomp and Circumstance, Ken called out the names of GREASE alumni and one by one each left their seat and joined the others onstage. Included were Treat Williams, John Travolta, Patrick Swayze and, although not a Broadway alumnus, but a "Greaser" none the less, Olivia Newton-John.

Joe Stein, author of FIDDLER ON THE ROOF, the previous title holder, came up onstage and said he was sorry he told everyone he knew to run and see GREASE. Ken and Maxine received a silver cup from the Guinness Book of World Records. Director Tom Moore, Choreographer Patricia Birch and Authors Jim Jacobs and Warren Casey all made speeches.

Following the historic performance, 3,000 people were entertained at the Sheraton Center. Chubby Checker performed. Food and drinks abounded. At 2 a.m., at the other end of the ballroom, the walls parted to reveal a Country and Western band and a huge country breakfast buffet. The dancing and celebrating went on until 6 a.m. and those who stayed to the end received a large button stating "I went the distance with GREASE!

It was an achievement that had taken continued enthusiasm, endurance, leadership, salesmanship, nerve and shrewdness, but being able to share the occasion with so many friends from my childhood up to the present is what gave the evening it's true meaning."

Early in the show's run, GREASE was picked up by Samuel French, the play publisher who makes it possible for universities, summer theatres, and high schools around the country to put on shows. Although Samuel French paid the highest price for a musical, at that time, to be able to act as agents for GREASE, they were greatly restricted from releasing rights to present the show as long as GREASE was planning to send touring companies around the country. When they negotiated for the rights, Samuel French only expected GREASE to run a little while longer giving them their full rights in a short period of time.

Ken and Maxine had demonstrated that they were entrepreneurs of the first rank.

December 8, 1979, GREASE becomes the longest running musical in Broadway history to date.

CHAPTER ELEVEN

The preceding chapters have recounted in specific detail the shows that Ken Waissman and Maxine Fox produced as a team. In the late 1970's, for the young professionals enrolled in IASTA-Northwood's Musical Theatre Studio and later in their Actors Ladder at the Players Club, Ken and Maxine answered questions and talked about producing.

"What does a producer do?" asked one of the enrolled actors.

Ken replied, "A producer is a master salesman. He sells the author on giving him the right to do a script; he sells a director on directing it; he sells stars on appearing in it; he sells investors on backing it; he sells a theatre owner on giving him a theatre; he works with the press people and the advertising people on how to sell it to the public to get them interested in it; and, if it's a flop, he sells his home, his mother, and his wife."

Ken added, pausing, "He does a lot. I think that producing is a gift and a talent, just like acting or directing. A producer has to be a catalyst, as well."

There are two kinds of producers. There are producers known in the business as presenters; there are producers known in the business as creative producers. A presenter is someone who may see a show on the West End, in London, or he may see a show in Louisville, Kentucky, and thinks there's a Broadway audience for that show. A presenter picks up the show and moves it to Broadway. He is not really involved in the creation of the show.

"A creative producer," Ken explained, "is someone who says, 'That's a good idea or script. Let's create a production.' If it's an idea for a show that the producer has, or an idea given to the producer, then he will have to choose who is going to write it."

That happens often on musicals. Who will compose?; who will do the lyrics?" interjects Maxine.

"Thus," continues Ken, "the producer is ever on the lookout for a script or a showcase of a show which interests him, excites him, and convinces him that it's a show, potentially, that could be a success. Of all the people who work in a show, the producer is the only one who is really involved in every aspect of the production."

"Perhaps you are wondering why Ken has not mentioned the 'money.'" Comments Maxine, "Raising the money is only about 25% of what we do."

"Yes, it's a small part," says Ken. "It is a small part in the overall picture, but it has to be done. Without the money, there's no production. That doesn't mean that raising money is something you do with the snap of a finger. It's a very major and time consuming aspect of producing."

"The only area in which I felt I was not respected because I was a woman," says Maxine, "was in raising money. I felt a very obvious dismissal of my role as a producer. When we were seeking financing men seemed always to focus on Ken; they'd dismiss me. It made me angry."

Maxine continues, "The investor can lose all the money he's invested in a show; he has to be prepared for that. But, he can also make a killing, getting a return on his money over a very long period of time, for eighteen years beyond the close of the last first-class company. Moreover, he may get his money back relatively quickly.

"It's a fun investment; reading the theatrical journal VARIETY (rather than The Wall Street Journal) to see how your money is doing. Our appeal to investors was not to their vanity, but to the pleasure it gives investing in Broadway. He or she can enjoy being a part of Broadway."

Ken interjects, "It's said that the producer 'foots the bill.' Well, the producer finds the people to 'foot the bill.' But the producer is personally libel for every dollar spent over the investment committed to the production. If the show runs over budget (we know of instances where shows have run way over budget), a producer is personally libel for that money. If the show goes over budget, and if he can't find anybody to come in at the last minute with the amount of money needed, the producer has to put the money into the show himself. Moreover, once the show has formally opened, if the show goes over budget and the money isn't there to pay the bills, the show closes.

CHAPTER ELEVEN

"What has become a very big thing in the last ten years or so is that a producer will go to what is called a showcase. Showcases are productions done in basements in New York, or in other parts of the country. They may be given by amateur performers or professional performers. Showcases in New York generally run about ten performances in the course of three weekends. It is a chance for the author to see his work on its feet, and hopefully, it will attract the interest of a producer. There's usually minimal scenery, but of late there has been a tendency for productions to become more elaborate and costly. From the showcase, the producer gets the basic substance for a Broadway show, the book and music."

Ken continues, "The first thing a producer must do, after he has a script, is to get a director, and then he and the director agree upon a choreographer and a musical director. The director will be in charge of everything that is going to happen on the stage; he will be involved in the casting. He is usually the main person in the casting of the show. He is very often not involved in the casting of a star. The star is the producer's prerogative — and problem. However, when it comes to all other aspects of the show, it is a team effort in which the director is the captain. For our production of GREASE, the producers auditioned the actors with the writers, the choreographer, the musical director, and, of course, the director. In summation, the director plans the show; he envisions how it will be set up on the stage, 'the blocking.' Concurrently, he has collaborated with the choreographer as to how the musical numbers should be staged, what the basic reasons for the numbers are which he or she is trying to get from what the composers have written.

"The producer then hires the set designer and costume designer in collaboration with the director. It is very important that the director see eye to eye and be able to get along with the costume designer and the set designer.

"The producer is also, at the same time, concerned with the other side of the coin: who is going to be the general business manager. Every show has a general manager. The general manager prepares the budget and is totally responsible for the finances of the production. He has got to keep the show on a budget; he has to make sure that the payroll is met every week when the show is running. The producer has the general manager on the one side, and the director on the other side of the coin. The general manager doesn't want to spend any money, because the best way to stay on budget is to have the entire budget there, unspent. The general manager screams one thing while the director screams, 'We want all the budget, and more.' The director is convinced that the budget should be double what it is. The costume designer thinks he has two-fifths of the budget, but needs three-fifth's for the costumes, while the set designer thinks half the budget is for his sets. The musical director wants a full orchestra, at least. Each involved in putting the show together thinks his department is the most important. That's not a bad thing," Ken was quick to say, "because each then gives his or her best to make the musical a hit."

"Such thinking on the part of each," added Maxine, "is important. The fact that everybody of the show thinks his or her area is the only area, the most important area, (even though it results in conflict), results in extra elements, contributions to the show."

"The producer however, has to be very selective of the co-workers he chooses, so their vision of the show coincides with his. There is no worse dilemma than for the show to arrive out of town with the producer seeing it one way and the director another way," added Ken.

"The producer is the final authority, and he has to resolve differences. The general manager often is willing to settle for one thing, while the director presses for something more spectacular.

"The producer has also selected a press representative to convey the image and the idea of the show to the public. He has engaged the services of an advertising agency which will be promoting the show.

"He is also responsible for selecting the theater, and the theater very often will play a very important part in how the show will actually look. Some shows are just too big for a small theater, or, too small for a big theater. There are some shows that are designed for small off-Broadway theatres, 200 seats, 300 seats. There is a certain charm in an intimate theater, watching a show like YOU'RE A GOOD MAN, CHARLIE BROWN, which was a big hit. It moved to Broadway, and immediately closed. The whole atmosphere had changed. Audience expectations uptown had likely been for a big musical.

"In tryouts (and previews) there are always surprises. No matter how well prepared everybody has been, things happen which have not been anticipated. The first performance in Philadelphia — or the first preview of the show in New York — the musical may seem a disaster.

CHAPTER ELEVEN

"Places where you had thought the audience was going to applaud, they just sat there stone-faced. Places where you had thought the audience was not going to respond, they laughed. Scenery that had been carefully worked seemed not to work, killed the timing; costumes, so carefully designed and fitted, required changes; setting up backstage for scene changes was deadly slow; songs that you had thought were going to be sending the audience up the aisles humming them at intermission were duds! The most important thing for a producer to do when the show is out of town is to make sure that everybody stays together, that they continue to communicate, that they remember why they got together in the first place.

"In recent years, showcases have been used in lieu of out-of-town tryouts, which was the pattern formerly. I still prefer the taking of the show out of town to find out where the bugs are. Costs of these showcase musicals, in New York and elsewhere, have escalated fantastically.

"I get the feeling after the first performance out of town that I've walked into a room that is totally in chaos. In a totally messy room, you must begin. You pick up one sock. After you've picked up one sock, then you right the chair. Before you know it, the whole room is cleaned up. Sometimes it's the producer who has to give that little goose to get people to pick up the first sock, to get everybody focused."

"It is an incredibly painful experience for the producer if the show does not become a hit." said Maxine.

"But let's say we have a hit," spoke up Ken enthusiastically, "and that it has settled into a run on Broadway.

"The way we work, not a week would go by that we wouldn't have a meeting with our press department, publicity department, and advertising department so as to make sure the name of the show stays in front of the public.

"There are three things that the producer should be concerned about supervising while the show is running. One is to keep the show as fresh as it was on opening night. You do that by hiring stage managers who have great directorial sensitivity, who know how the show is put together and who can keep the director's work on the same level that it was when the show opened. That is very, very important. Also, as a producer, you hope to have a strong relationship with your director so he or she will come back occasionally and work with the actors and the replacements.

"If it's a musical, the choreographer should come back every few months or so and do brush up rehearsals; hence, a relationship should be fostered with the choreographer so that you can pick up the phone and say (in our case it was Patricia Birch), 'Pat, the hand-jive number is starting to loosen. You better get down here.' Pat may be involved with other things, but she'll say, 'Okay, let's see: Thursday from 4:30 to 6 I'll be there. Tell the stage manager.'

"She gets everybody on stage and cleans up a routine that had gotten a little sloppy."

"We all cared. Cared that GREASE maintain the high level of performance that it had established in the first weeks of the run." added Maxine.

"After each performance we wanted every member of the audience to go out and talk to twenty people the next day about the show they had seen the night before. It's the producers' job to make sure that tickets sell, that the show runs longer. Enthusiastic word of mouth after each performance is reflected six months later.

"Two, it's important to keep selling what you have produced. There was an attitude on Broadway for many, many years that once a show had opened: that was it. Not another effort. Not a new pair of shoes; not another rehearsal; not a change of a light bulb. Nothing. That was not a totally impractical point of view. In the '20's and '30's, the runs weren't very long. It was only 3 months; maybe a year.

"In our case, based on our assumption of a long run, we would give the stage manager a list of notes to pass on to the cast. We'd tell him if we saw something not working. It would be his job to find out how to solve what was wrong.

"There were times when we'd catch a performance, and we'd say to each other, 'If this trend keeps up, the audiences will eventually notice that the show's not up to par. If this continues, the show is going to get seedy, or it's going to look tired.' At that point, we'd ask our director, Tom Moore, to come back for a look. We'd bring Pat in.

"We go to our show every week or two. Whenever we see that things are being put into the show by cast members, certain little 'improvements' that are not supposed to be there, we try correcting the situation through the stage manager, who gives the cast notes.

"After one performance, an actor in the cast came up to me and said, 'You know, we weren't up to par last night! You had a right to be upset, but last night there was standing room only, so what difference did it make?' "

Ken continued recounting the incident, having said to the actor, "They paid money to see you give your best performance. Just because we're sold out was no reason to thumb your nose at them.

"Equally important is the fact that the performances you gave in May resulted in there being audiences in December. Tonight's performance does not bring in tomorrow night's audience; it was performances of a year ago that will fill the house tomorrow night. The performance you gave tonight affects the size of the house six months from now; your bad performance will be felt six months from now. The actor said, 'I never thought of it that way.' "

"GREASE had some risque language in it; some 1950's gestures. The cast had begun to throw more vulgarities in. Rude gestures are easy to come by; they're cheap; they get a cheap laugh. Little by little, such had crept in. We'd gotten upset with this padding. We told the stage manager to go back to the prompt script, to get everything out that wasn't written there. We pointed out to our stage manager that when an actor makes an obscene gesture that doesn't belong, that he is doing something that the authors did not write, that the director did not direct, that the producers did not plan having in their show. Somebody may not buy a ticket because their neighbor saw a show that had offended them.

"Four years into the run, the show started to look tired. Nothing was getting it back to a pristine performance. Finally, we sat down with Tom and Pat and said, 'Okay, let's just get rid of this cast.'

"We made an announcement that nobody in that show had to be there, that no one was forcing them to be in the show. If they did not like coming to the theater; if they didn't like performing with each other; if they were bored, they did not have to be there!

"They were given three days to think about whether they wanted to be there or not.

"Tom, Pat, Maxine and I decided to talk to each member of the company, individually. By the third day, we had called each one of them into the office. Some we told that we felt it would be better if they weren't in the show. Of some, we asked what was wrong, saying,

'Why are you putting us in a position of wanting you not to be in the show?'

"They hated what was said to them, but it really put energy back into the show. They had forgotten that they liked being actors, that they liked each other, that they liked having a theater to come to, that they liked an audience there every night.

"They came prepared to work at rehearsals. Suddenly, they had found it was exciting to be in GREASE. No one was replaced."

Maxine added, "As producers we respect our audiences. The minute you lose sight of that you take months and months off your run."

Ken recapitulated thus, "The first thing is maintaining the show the way it looked on opening night. That's the producer's responsibility, and he needs to keep in the cast the very best people available. Continuity is important.

"Sometimes actors forget the agent works for them, and not the other way around. Meg Bennett was in the show for about a year and a half. One day she came up and made an appointment to see us. She came in, sat down, and said, 'It took me a while to build up the courage to talk to you; I've been with the show now for over a year and a half; I thought you liked my performance.'

"Her story was that she couldn't understand why we were giving raises to everybody around her, but we were keeping her on minimum.

"We told her that it was her agent's doing, saying, 'Meg, we'd like to give you that raise, but our policy has been that we do not put an actor above minimum unless he's on a 3-month contract; that's the only way we, as producers, know that two weeks from now that performer in GREASE is going to be on that stage. For that, we pay the extra money.'

"Well, I certainly plan to stay with the show for at least the next six months.'

"Meg's agent had been very emphatic with us that she wanted this young lady on a two-week minimum contract. The actress had not been told this.

"In regard to actors," Ken continued, "We saw hundreds of people for the original GREASE cast. For each company that we put together after that, we saw almost as many. We auditioned a lot of talented people, but either they didn't fit the role we were casting, or,

CHAPTER ELEVEN

Richard Gere

Ken Waissman & Jeff Conway

CHAPTER ELEVEN

though they may have been terrific as actors, often they couldn't sing, or, they could sing but they could not act. We weren't looking for trained dancers, but some who auditioned couldn't move at all. It was often very frustrating. Actors dread auditions. We do too.

"We remembered when Treat Williams first came in to audition. That was one of his first auditions in his career. We thought he was talented. We decided to put him on as an understudy and see if he would grow. Treat Williams later came and took over the lead, Danny Zuko, on Broadway.

"Richard Gere came to audition in an open call. (Actors Equity, some years ago, had ruled that for each new Broadway production, there should be a day set aside as an open call; that means a call to which, in great numbers, young actors and actresses, who may not have an Equity union card, and usually don't, can come and audition. (Among the actors in New York, it is often referred to as a 'cattle call' for the hoards of actors assembling, early in the morning, outside the stage door of the Broadway theatre or the rehearsal hall where the call is being held.) We liked Gere. He was new to New York. Pat Birch went up on stage to start showing him a few dance steps; abruptly Richard Gere walked right off the stage and out the stage door. We thought, 'How odd. He sang well and read well.'

"Linda Otto, who was then our casting director, said, 'I don't understand this. Suddenly to walk off in front of everybody, just walk offstage. No comment. Nothing. And then out the door.'

"Linda called him and learned that he had been scared to death of a dance audition. It was explained to him that Pat Birch liked to work with actors, who might not be dancers, if they could move well. He came back a few weeks later, and he was marvelous. So, we hired him to understudy. Most of these people we cast started as understudies. Jeff Conaway was still a student at New York University when we hired him to understudy."

Maxine and Ken had traveled to the West Coast, and John Travolta had found out that they were auditioning for a company of GREASE.

"I want to audition for GREASE." said John Travolta to casting directors Linda Otto and Geri Winzor. John had traveled from New York to California to visit his sisters, Ellen and Annie, both working actresses. Linda Otto thought that John Travolta was too young to audition. Travolta persisted.

John Travolta

CHAPTER ELEVEN

Travolta's manager called. "Wouldn't you just see him?"

Again, Linda said, "He's very young and we really aren't hiring anybody that inexperienced."

Travolta countered with, "I'll help out in the office. And he did. He helped run the mimeograph machine and was a 'go-fer' (one who goes for coffee, etc.).

All succumbed to Travolta's innocence and charm.

Finally, Linda Otto said, "Okay, John, we'll let you audition; it will be for Ken, Maxine, Pat Birch, Tom Moore, and the authors, Jim and Warren."

Ken remembers, "The minute he walked out onstage, we four were absolutely fascinated. He read well; his instincts were terrific."

Ken also remembers saying to Tom, "Do you think he really could sustain eight performances a week? He doesn't have much experience, only stock, nothing professional."

Tom said, "I think he could. His instincts are so good. I really think it's worth the gamble."

"All four of us agreed," said Ken. So, John Travolta was hired to be in the first national company of GREASE.

Ken had said that one can not really replace somebody on the road, while touring; that it was taking a big risk, therefore, to hire a young and inexperienced actor, if he doesn't work out. It was a real gamble.

"Travolta loved airplanes," Ken related. "The company manager's job to book all the reservations and move everybody around from place to place interested John Travolta. The company manager discovered that John knew every airline schedule. If you wanted to know what flights there were out of Chicago, you just asked him. He seemed to know everything. It ended up with Travolta's making all the flight arrangements for the whole touring cast.

"One day John and I were standing onstage, and I was kidding him. I said, 'Do you want to be an actor or a company manager?' He said, 'I just like making flight arrangements.'

"The innocence he had in the role of Doody, he also seemed to have offstage. He was both innocent and, in those days, a little 'klutzy.' We were sitting in Charlie's Restaurant, one day in New York, and John walked in and waved, banged into the wall and knocked over two chairs."

MAKING A BROADWAY MUSICAL

Jerry Zaks, Michael Lembeck, Jeff Conway, Candice Early in the first national company of GREASE.

CHAPTER ELEVEN

John Travolta didn't play the lead in the national company. He played Danny Zuko's sidekick Doody: the innocent kid who is sort of married to his guitar. He sings Magic Changes.

Ken added, "Travolta played Doody on the road for a year. Then, we brought him to New York, and he played the role on Broadway for a while."

In addition to finding and nurturing large numbers of actors and actresses who became stars, Ken and Maxine managed to get an eight-and-a-half-year run for GREASE.

The members of the IASTA-Northwood Musical Theatre Studio were fascinated by every aspect of their careers, and one of them, getting back to basics, asked, "What is it like getting started in this business?" Ken replied, "Everyone involved in Broadway is there because he or she has one thing in mind, this business. If you have any alternative, take it, because this is not an easy profession."

Ken ended with, "I do believe that if an actor, producer, director, anybody ambitious for a career in the theater, has determination, discipline, talent, and a willingness to grow, they can make their way, regardless of the fact that there is very little encouragement, and very little help from anyone."

Ken Waissman & Judy Kaye

RESIDUUM

The thought that emerges from my telling the lives of Ken Waissman and Maxine Fox as entrepreneurs is that young, creative people in America can still beat the system into which the commercial Broadway theatre has drifted.

Ken had this to say about entrepreneurship: "You have to be creative and a catalyst. I think my definition of entrepreneur is: he's a showman. When he's trying to fill a 1,500 to 2,000 seat house on Broadway (or on the road), as an entrepreneur, he has to be very strong, with instinctual convictions, decisive about going forward. And, being flexible is extremely important."

The price is likely to be great, as has been seen. However, Phoenix-like, both Maxine and Ken have risen again and will be able to rise above any commercial setbacks.

They became rich, Sardi celebrities, admired by all the young performers they had nurtured. The first GREASE "find" to be tapped for TV stardom was Adrienne Barbeau. GREASE alumni Meg Bennett, Ilene Kristen, Candice Early, and John Driver found roles in soap operas. Of course, the most sensational successes the musical spawned were in motion pictures: John Travolta, Richard Gere, Marilu Henner, Treat Williams, Barry Bostwick and Patrick Swayze.

Judy Kaye, recipient of two Tony Awards, Walter Charles, and Joel Higgens, continue to distinguish themselves as performers. Jerry Zaks, turning to directing, won a Tony Award and has piled up an impressive number of stage successes including the Lincoln Center revival of ANYTHING GOES.

Ever since GREASE and OVER HERE!, Tom Moore has continually been in demand on Broadway and at regional theatres. He directed the hit Broadway revival of ONCE IN A LIFE TIME and the Pulitzer Prize-winning play 'NIGHT MOTHER for which he also di-

Jerry Zaks & Maxine Fox

rected the film version. Currently, he is directing the hit television series L.A. LAW.

Patricia Birch went on from GREASE to do the musical staging for A LITTLE NIGHT MUSIC, CANDIDE, THEY'RE PLAYING OUR SONG, and PACIFIC OVERTURES. She directed the musical numbers in the film version of GREASE and directed the sequel. She recently won an Emmy Award for staging the television tribute to George Gershwin which starred Mikhail Barishnikov among others.

Authors Jim Jacobs and Warren Casey have never regretted leaving Chicago and their 'day jobs.' They have written feature films, done workshop productions and collaborated with other writers. Jacobs married Denise Nettleton who played the role of 'Marty' in GREASE on tour and later in New York. They reside in Redondo Beach, California. Warren passed on in 1989. GREASE alumni from both coasts sent their condolences and many were able to fly to Chicago for his memorial ceremony.

It's interesting to contemplate how different so many lives would have been if not for the enthusiasm, endurance, conclusiveness, leadership ability, sales ability, nerve and shrewdness of Ken Waissman and Maxine Fox. That's entrepreneurship!

EPILOGUE

In the beginning of 1980, Ken and Maxine went their separate ways. They were divorced in the fall of that year. They began as two youngsters from Baltimore determined to conquer a place for themselves in the world of Broadway. The success, celebrity, and passing years resulted in new priorities and interests for each.

Among other things, Ken has produced two of the 1980's most successful long-running dramas, AGNES OF GOD, which starred Elizabeth Ashley, Geraldine Page and Amanda Plummer, and TORCH SONG TRILOGY, which won a Tony Award in 1983 as Best Play and earned Ken a personal Tony Award as Producer. The screen version of AGNES OF GOD stars Jane Fonda and the screen version of TORCH SONG TRILOGY stars Harvey Fierstein, Ann Bancroft, and Matthew Broderick. Ken is currently preparing a stage play based on the film THE DAYS OF WINE & ROSES.

Maxine remarried and is now Maxine Fox Lorence. She developed several musicals for the commercial theatre and, in the process, became alarmed at the damage to the musical theatre being caused by the new ways of raising money. Massive budgets in the millions of dollars had created new power bases that had no knowledge of theatre craft. As a result good, entertaining, well-produced musicals rarely made it to a Broadway opening night — greatly reducing the normally shocking odds for success.

Rather than keep banging her head against that musical brick wall, Maxine has gone off in search of answers. Based on her past record, I have a feeling she'll find them. Stay tuned!

SELECTED BIBLIOGRAPHY

Abbott, George. "Mister Abbott". New York: Random House, 1963.

Avis, Warren. Take A Chance To Be First. New York: Macmillan, 1986.

Belz, Carl. The Story Of Rock. New York: Oxford University Press, 1969.

Brown, Deaver. The Entrepreneur's Guide. New York: Ballantine, 1981.

Burton, Jack. Blue Book Of Broadway Musicals. New York: Century House, 1952.

Callow, Simon. Being an Actor. London: Methuen, 1984.

Coffee, R. & Scase, R. Women In Charge: Experience of Female Entrepreneurs. London: Allen Unwin, 1985.

Cook, James R. The Start-Up Entrepreneur. New York: Harper & Rowe, 1987.

Dunn, Don. The Making of No, No, Nanette. Secaucus, N.J.: Citadel Press, 1972.

Durcker, Peter. In Search of Excellence: Managing in Turbulent Times. New York: Harper & Rowe 1980

Eells, George. The Life That He Led: A Biography of Cole Porter. New York: G.P. Putnam's Sons, 1967.

Engel, Lehman. Getting Started In The Theater. New York: Collier Books, A division of Macmillan Publications Company, 1973.

Engel, Lehman. Words With Music. New York: Macmillan Company, 1972.

Engel, Lehman. The American Musical Theatre: A Consideration In Planning & Producing The Musical Show.

Engel, Lehman. Their Words Are Music (The Great Theatre Lyricists And Their Lyrics). New York: Crown Publishers, Inc., 1975.

Ewen, David. The American Musical Theatre. New York: Henry Holt & Company, 1958.

Gershwin, Ira. Lyrics On Several Occasions. New York: Alfred A. Knoph, 1959.

Green, Stanley. The World Of Musical Comedy. New York: Zif-Davis, 1960.

Hammerstein, Oscar, II. Lyrics. New York: Simon & Schuster, 1949.

Harburg, E. Y. At This Point In Rhyme. New York: Crown Publishers, Inc. 1976.

King, Larry. The Whorehouse Papers. New York: Viking Press, 1982.

Lambro, Donald. Land of Opportunity: The Entrepreneurial Spirit In America. New York: Little, 1986.

Laufe, Abe. Broadway's Greatest Musicals (Revised Ed.). New York: Funk & Wagnalls, 1977.

Loney, Glenn, ed. Musical Theatre in America: Papers and Proceedings in America. Westport, CT: Greenwood, 1984.

McCormach, Mark H. What They Don't Teach You At Harvard Business School. New York, Bantam, 1984.

Rado, James & Ragni, Gerome. Hair. New York: Pocketbooks, 1969.

Reed, Joseph Verner. The Curtain Falls. New York: Harcourt, Brace and Company, 1935.

Rodgers & Hart Songbook, The. New York: Simon & Schuster, 1951.

Wilk, Max. Every Day's a Matinee. New York: W.W. Norton & Company, Inc., 1975.

MATERIALS AND BACKGROUND

Bordman, Gerald. American Musical Theatre: A Chronicle. New York: Oxford U. Press, 1978.

Gorer, Geoffrey. The American People: A Study in National Character. New York: W.W. Norton & Company, Inc., 1948.

Mitchell, J. D. "Contemporary American Theatre . . . a psychologic sounding board." Natya, Theatre Arts Journal. New Delhi: Spring, 1960.

MUSIC

The American Musical Theatre. Columbia Records 32-B5-004. With book by Lehman Engel and Introduction by Brooks Atkinson.
An Evening with Johnny Mercer, Allan Jay Lerner, Sheldon Harnick. Laureate Records LL-601 LL-602 Ll-603.

VIDEO CASSETTE

CAREER PREPARATION FOR THE MUSICAL THEATRE, 35 minutes.
    (Available from IASTA)

OTHER MATERIALS AVAILABLE FROM IASTA

Films - Video Cassettes - Books

FILMS

(All films are in 16mm and are available on BETA and VHS cassette.)

*ASPECTS OF THE CLASSIC GREEK THEATRE, 13 minutes.
EURIPEDES' LIFE AND TIMES: THE TROJAN WOMEN, 38 minutes
ROMAN COMEDY, PT. I, 22 minutes.
(Scenes from Plautus' **Amphitryon** and Shakespeare's **A Comedy of Errors**)
ROMAN COMEDY, PT. II, 24 minutes
(Scenes from Terence's **Phormio** and Molière's **Scapin**)
*ITALY: ORIGINS OF THEATRE TO PIRANDELLO, 20 minutes.
*MEDIEVAL THEATRE, 16 minutes
*ASPECTS OF THE COMMEDIA DELL'ARTE, 14 minutes
*THE GREEN BIRD, 35 minutes.
(Carlo Gozzi's *commedia* classic)
*SHAKESPEARE'S THEATRE AND MACBETH, 16 minutes.
SHAKESPEARE'S KING LEAR AND THE MIDDLE AGES, 31 minutes.
SHAKESPEARE AND WEBSTER: JACOBEAN ENGLAND, 33 minutes.
PARABLES OF POWER, PT. I, 40 minutes.
(Scenes from Shakespeare's **Henry VIII**)
PARABLES OF POWER, PT. II, 45 minutes.
(Scenes from Marlowe's **Edward II**)
PARABLES OF POWER, PT. III, 50 minutes.
(Scenes from Marlowe's **Tamburlaine** and **Dr. Faustus**)
THE SPANISH GOLDEN AGE OF THEATRE, PT. I, 38 minutes.
(Scenes from Lopé de Vega's **Knight From Olmedo**)
THE SPANISH GOLDEN AGE OF THEATRE, PT. II, 26 minutes.
(Scenes from Calderón de la Barca's **Phantom Lady**)
*MOLIÈRE AND THE COMÉDIE FRANÇAISE, 17 minutes.
*ASPECTS OF THE NEO-CLASSIC THEATRE, 13 minutes.
(Scenes from Racine's **Phèdre**)

SHERIDAN'S 18TH CENTURY ENGLAND, PT.I, 33 minutes.
   (Scenes from **The Rivals**)
SHERIDAN'S 18TH CENTURY ENGLAND, PT. II, 36 minutes.
   (Scenes from **The School for Scandal**)
*ASPECTS OF THE 19TH CENTURY COMEDY, 12 minutes.
PARIS AND THE 19TH CENTURY NOVELISTS, 26 minutes.
   (Balzac, Flaubert, Dumas, Stendhal, Hugo, George Sands, Zola)
IBSEN'S LIFE AND TIMES, PT. I, 28 minutes.
   (Youth and Self-Imposed Exile)
IBSEN'S LIFE AND TIMES, PT. II, 24 minutes.
   (The Later Years)
ENGLAND'S WRITERS OF THE 19TH CENTURY, 36 minutes.
   (Wordsworth, Byron, the Brownings, Keats, Shelley, Wilde, Tennyson)
GEORGE BERNARD SHAW AND HIS TIMES, 35 minutes.
*IRISH THEATRE & JUNO AND THE PAYCOCK, 16 minutes.
*CHEKHOV AND THE MOSCOW ART THEATRE, 13 minutes.
*GERMAN THEATER: BRECHT AND SCHILLER, 32 minutes.

ASIAN THEATRE FILMS

*SANSKRIT DRAMA, 14 minutes.
*THE STYLE OF THE CLASSIC JAPANESE NOH THEATRE, 17 minutes.
*ASPECTS OF THE KABUKI THEATRE OF JAPAN, 12 minutes.
*ASPECTS OF PEKING OPERA, 15 minutes.
*MARTIAL ARTS OF PEKING OPERA, 12 minutes.
   (black and white)

FOREIGN LANGUAGE FILMS

*GERMAN THEATER: BRECHT & SCHILLER, 16 minutes.
    (German soundtrack)
PARIS AND THE 19TH CENTURY NOVELISTS, 26 minutes.
    (French soundtrack)
*THE SPANISH GOLDEN AGE OF THEATRE, 13 minutes.
    (Spanish soundtrack)

*CONTAIN ARCHIVE FOOTAGE FROM IASTA PRODUCTIONS

OTHER BOOKS BY THE AUTHOR

Published by Northwood Press

THEATRE: THE SEARCH FOR STYLE
ACTORS TALK: ABOUT STYLES OF ACTING
THE GREEN BIRD
THE FOX CAT (Substituted for the Crown Prince)
MACBETH UNJINXED
JEAN RACINE'S PHÈDRE ON STAGE
THE STAGING OF A SPANISH CLASSIC: THE HOUSE OF FOOLS
    (Publication Spring 1990)

ORDERS AND INQUIRIES

The Institute for Advanced Studies in the Theatre Arts
IASTA
12 West End Avenue, Room 304
New York, NY 10023
(212) 581-3133
Toll Free Number
(Outside New York)
1 (800) 843-8334

INDEX

A

A JOYFUL NOISE 39–40, 57
A LITTLE NIGHT MUSIC 113
Abbott, George 43–44, 63
Actors Equity 51, 67–68, 81, 105
Actors Ladder 95
AGNES OF GOD 67, 115
Allen, Rae 48–49
Alone At A Drive-In Movie 56
Ambassador Theatre 72
AND MISS REARDON DRINKS A LITTLE .... xvii, 48, 51
Andrews Sisters .... ix–x, xvii, 77–81
Andrews, Maxene 77–81
Andrews, Patti 77–81
ANYTHING GOES 111
Ashley, Elizabeth 115

B

Bakshi, Ralph 83
Bancroft, Ann 115
Barbeau, Adrienne .... xvi, 111
Barishnikov, Mikhail 113
Barnes, Clive 45, 66–67
Barr, Richard 70

Beauty School Dropout 51, 53, 91
Bennet, Michael 39, 57
Bennett, Meg 102, 111
Birch, Patricia .... xvi, 57, 59, 61–64, 75, 93, 100–101, 105, 107, 113
Bobbie, Walter 91
Bogotá, Colombia 24, 26, 28–29
BONNIE AND CLYDE 48
BORN YESTERDAY 2
Boston University 19
Bostwick, Barry .... xvi, 91, 111
Broadhurst Theatre .... xvii, 72–73
Broderick, Matthew 115
Burton, Richard 35

C

CANDIDE 113
CARNIVAL 20
Caro, Warren 72–73
Carr, Allan 83–85
Casey, Warren .... xvi, 51, 53–54, 56, 59, 61, 63–64, 93, 107, 113
Channing, Carol 79
Charles, Walter 111
Checker, Chubby 93
Cohen, Alexander H. 69–70
Conaway, Jeff .... xvi, 91, 105

D

Daily News (NY) 66–67
DAYS OF WINE AND ROSES, THE 115
Demas, Carole 91
Driver, John 111

E

Early, Candice .... xvi, 91, 111
Eden Theatre .... ix, xvi, 62, 66, 68, 73
EDUCATION OF HYMAN KAPLAN, THE 43–44
Elliot, Cass 43

F

FIDDLER ON THE ROOF	ix, xvi, 91, 93
Fierstein, Harvey	115
FIG LEAVES ARE FALLING, THE	44
FINIAN'S RAINBOW	1–3
FOOTLIGHT FEVER	13–15
FORTUNE AND MEN'S EYES	xv, xvii, 45–46, 51
46th Street Theatre	1–3
Fosse, Bob	36
Freedman, Gerald	59
FRITZ, THE CAT	83
Fryer, Carr, and Harris	36, 38
FUNNY GIRL	21–22, 31–33, 35, 39

G

Gere, Richard	xvi, 105, 111
Gershwin, George	113
Gould, Elliot	36
Grauman's Chinese Theatre	87
GREASE	ix–x, xv–xviii, 27, 29–30, 39, 51,53–54, 56–57, 59, 61–64, 66–70, 72–73, 75, 78, 83–85, 87, 89, 91, 93, 97, 100–102, 105, 107, 109, 111, 113
Grease Lightnin'	53
Gross, Shelly	19, 21
Guber, Lee	19, 21

H

HAIR	59
Hand Jive	56
Harburg, Yip	3
Harris, Julie	xvii, 48–49
Harris, Sylvia	36
Heckart, Eileen	48
Henner, Marilu	xvi, 89, 91, 111
Higgens, Joel	111
Holt, Will	77
Houseman, John	61
Hunt, Betty Lee	36, 38, 69–70

I

ICM (International Creative Management) 56–57, 84
Incamp, Klaus 89
IRENE 78

J

Jacobs, Bernard 80
Jacobs, Jim .... xvi, 51, 53–54, 56, 59, 61, 63, 93, 107, 113

K

Kanin, Garson 21–22, 31–33
Kaye, Judy .... xvi, 91, 111
Kerr, Walter 45
KISS ME KATE 13
Kristen, Ilene .... xvi, 91, 111

L

L.A. LAW 113
LA CASA DE MUSICA (MUSIC HOUSE) 25–29
Lansbury, Angela 38
Lawrence, Lawrence Shubert 72–73
League of American Theatres and Producers 70
League of New York Theatres 68–70
Lembeck, Michael 91
Lennart, Isobel 31
LORELEI 79
LOVE OF LIFE 43
Lucker, Bruce 89
Lyceum Theatre 70

M

MADWOMAN OF CHAILLOT, THE 19
Magic Changes 53, 109
MAME 38–39
Martin Beck Theatre 70
Mattsis, Ray De 91
May, Elaine 36
Mineo, Sal .... xv, xvii, 45–46
Monster Mash 56

Moore, Tom .... xvi, 45, 59, 61–64, 66, 75, 93, 100–101, 107, 111
Moss, Kathi..91
Musical Theatre Studio (IASTA-Northwood)......... xi, xv, 3, 67, 95, 109

N

Nettleton, Denise 113
Neuwald, Ellen 45
New York Post 67
New York University..23, 43, 105
Newton-John, Olivia .... xvii, 89, 91, 93
'NIGHT MOTHER 111
Northwood Institute..x–xii, xv

O

off-Broadway 40, 57, 63, 68, 98
OKLAHOMA 2–3
ON YOUR TOES..44
ONCE IN A LIFE TIME... 111
Otto, Linda 105–107
OVER HERE! .... ix, xvii, 75, 78–81, 111

P

PACIFIC OVERTURES 113
Page, Geraldine 115
Page, Sharon 44
Palace Theatre 3, 36
Paramount Pictures .... xvii, 83–85, 87
Paramount Theatre..78
Parsons, Estelle..xvii, 48
Paul, Alan 91
Peace Corps 24–26, 28–29, 43, 91
PHANTOM OF THE OPERA 91
Phoenix Theatre 62
Plummer, Amanda 115

R

R. U. R. 19
Rehearsal Club 20, 33
Reynolds, Debbie 78
Robbins, Jerome...32
Royale Theatre ....xvii, 91

S

Saks, Gene 38
Salisbury, Leah...44
Samuel French, Inc. 93
SATURDAY NIGHT FEVER 84
Schary, Dore 40
SECRET STORM 43
Sherman Brothers..ix, 75, 77
Shubert Alley 78
Shubert Organization..70, 72, 80
Shubert Theatre ....xvii, 73, 78
Sinatra, Frank...35
Smith, Rex ....xvi, 91
STAGE DOOR 20
Stein, Joe...93
Stigwood, Robert..84–85
Streisand, Barbra 21–22, 32–33, 35–36
Styne, Jule 21
Summer Nights 55–56
Swayze, Patrick 91, 93, 111
SWEET CHARITY 36–39

T

THE ME NOBODY KNOWS...57
The New York Times..45, 54, 66
The Players 95
The Wall Street Journal 96
THEY'RE PLAYING OUR SONG 113
TORCH SONG TRILOGY..115
Travolta, John............... xvi–xvii, 84–85, 87, 89, 91, 93, 105, 107–109, 111
Tune, Tommy..39

INDEX

U
University of Maryland 12–17

V
VARIETY 44–46, 96
VASALINA 29
VICTORY CANTEEN 77

W
Watt, Doug 45
We Go Together 53
Weaver, Gordon 85
Weidman, Jerome 45
Whitelaw, Arthur 40–41
Williams, Treat .... xvi, 93, 105, 111
Winzor, Geri 105
Witt, Peter 77
Wittokur, Karen 44

Y
YOU'RE A GOOD MAN, CHARLIE BROWN 40–41, 57, 98

Z
Zaks, Jerry 91, 111
Zindel, Paul 48